Sexual Harassment in American Secondary Schools

Sexual Harassment in American Secondary Schools

A Legal Guide for Administrators, Teachers and Students

Nancy S. Layman, J.D.

Contemporary Research Press
Dallas / 1994

Library of Congress Cataloguing in Publication Data

Layman, Nancy S., 1942-
        Sexual harassment in American secondary schools: a legal guide for administrators, teachers, and students / Nancy S. Layman.
                p. cm.
        Includes bibliographical references and index.
        ISBN 0-935061-57-6 (cloth)
        ISBN 0-935061-52-5 (paper)
        1. Sex discrimination in education--Law and legislation--United States. 2. Education, Secondary--Law and legislation--United States. I. Title.
KF4155.L39   1993
344.73'0798--dc20
[347.304798]   93-11323
                                                CIP

ISBN 0-935061-57-6 (cloth)
ISBN 0-935061-52-5 (paper)

First published by Contemporary Research Press in 1994

Contemporary Research Press
P.O. Box 7240
Dallas, Texas 75209

Printed in the United States of America

10 9 8 7 6 5 4 3

To

My Mother, Eleanor Frances Staats
(1919 - 1957)

and

My Grandmother, Christina Mack Meyer
(1898 - 1980)

CONTENTS

Acknowledgments

Many thanks to all the people who unselfishly gave their time and who contributed to this book: Professors Jane Aiken and Thomas Haggard, University of South Carolina School of Law; M. Malissa Burnette, Esq., Gergel, Burnette, Nickles & Grant, P.A.; M. Jane Turner, Esq., Childs & Duff, P.A.; Martin Banks, Esq.; Mary Waters, South Carolina Commission on Women; Professor Miriam Freeman, University of South Carolina School of Social Work; Jemme Stewart, Counselor; Mary Sneed and Bobby Gist, South Carolina Human Affairs Commission; Nan Stein, Wellesley College Center for Research on Women; Professor James Sears, College of Education, University of South Carolina; Sue Sattel, Minnesota Sex Equity Specialist; Susan Davis, South Carolina Office of Occupational Education; Kathy Handel, Jane Doug Hyatt, and Pie White, Spring Valley High School, Columbia, South Carolina; Liz Brockington, Dreher High School, Columbia, South Carolina; W. Ben Nesbit, South Carolina Department of Education; Jim Taylor, Airport High School, West Columbia, South Carolina; Dr. Robert F. Sabalis, University of South Carolina School of Medicine.

And to my family, Rick, Abe, and Nick, for their love and support.

Introduction

Estimates are that only 5% or less of the United States population, both male and female, sexually harass other people. But the potential for physical and psychological damage to the victims of sexual harassment is great and the consequences may be permanent. Sexual harassment is not a separate, isolated phenomenon but is related to other forms of discrimination, such as that based on race, religion, or national origin. It is a display of power where the perpetrator attempts to exert control over another, and it manifests itself in disrespect and often hostility toward the victim. It is demonstrated in a classroom by gender discrimination when a math teacher says, "You girls will probably have a hard time understanding these binomial equations--they're really difficult." Or, when an English teacher says, "Girls and sensitive boys will like the poetry of Words-worth."

More overtly, it is seen when a boy grabs a girl's breast or tries to undo her bra strap. The underlying requirement for sexual harassment is that it not be consensual: the recipient must not desire or welcome the sexual advance.

Throughout this book, the harasser will usually be referred to as "he," since men are more likely to sexually harass than women. However, women are not exempt from harassing, and they, too, are subject to the same laws of discrimination as men. The laws also apply to same-sex harassment. Men who claim they would enjoy being sexually harassed often feel differently when their harasser is another man. The purpose of this book is to familiarize middle and high school administrators, teachers, and students with the laws implicated by sexual harassment and strategies for dealing with it. But, of course, familiarity with the law is insufficient to prevent sexual harassment. Knowledge of psychology, sociology, pedagogy, and child development will also aid teachers, administrators, and other school personnel in analyzing and helping to end sexual harassment.

In understanding this phenomenon of sexual harassment, it helps to keep in mind some of the common goals shared by schools: to develop each child to his or her potential; to create an environment in which teachers, students, and other employees are comfortable and safe; to provide a purposeful and challenging curriculum that meets the needs of the students as well as those of society; and to encourage the development of tolerance and respect for humankind. The two major federal Acts proscribing sex discrimination, Title VII and Title IX, are also intended to achieve specific goals: to insure equality and opportunity for women as well as men in both the workplace and in the schools. When bars exist to the achievement of any of these goals in the school environment, everyone loses: the students, the teachers, and the community-at-large. One such bar is sexual harassment.

The public has been inundated by the media with reports of sexual harassment. From television news programs to "Donahue" and after-school specials to news magazines and women's magazines, Americans have been preoccupied with the topic. Although laws forbidding discrimination based on sex had been in effect for over two decades, it wasn't until the Clarence Thomas Supreme Court confirmation hearings in 1991 that sexual harasssment was freely discussed. As law Professor Catherine MacKinnon has written, "It is not surprising. . .that women would not complain of an experience for which there has been no name. Until 1976, lacking a term to express it, sexual harassment was literally unspeakable, which made generalized, shared and social definitions of it inaccessible."[1] In that year a federal district court found that the discharge of a female employee for reject-ing the sexual advances of her male supervisor constituted sex discrimination in violation of Title VII of the Civil Rights Act. The decision in that case, *Williams v. Saxbe*[2], laid the foundation for federal case law recognizing sexual harassment as a form of sex discrimination prohibited by Title VII of The Civil Rights Act of 1964. In the following year, 1977, three federal courts of appeals reversed lower court decisions which had held that sexual harassment claims were not within the scope of Title VII.

At the Thomas confirmation hearings Anita Hill talked about her experiences of sexual harassment, and from that time forward, the subject has been discussed in living rooms and in board rooms, in offices and in schools, in bars and in churches. Not only has it been discussed, its parameters have been expanded. Recent scandals involving the military, in which women have spoken out about assaults that occurred during Operation Desert Storm and at the Navy's Tailhook party in Las Vegas, have kept the topic in front of an attentive and often perplexed public. Charges of sexual harassment have been made against a broad spectrum of workers--from Congressmen to day laborers. Publicity regarding the harassment of women doctors and nurses as well as those women working in previously all-male jobs, such as welding or road construction, has emphasized the pervasiveness of the problem. The president of the Associated Press Managing Editors stated that one of every three female journalists who responded to a survey asserted she has been sexually harassed in the newsroom where she works. In another study, six out of ten women lawyers reported they had been the target of unwanted sexual advances or other forms of sexual harassment in the last five years. Surveys of working women and of teenage girls reveal that more than half of them are being sexually harassed, many on a daily basis.

In addition, the public's attention has been directed, largely by the media, to other issues related to sexual harassment: child abuse and violence against women on the streets, on the campus, and in the home. Molestation of children by the clergy, by Boy Scout leaders, by teachers, and by daycare workers has added fuel to discussions. Laws now criminalize possession of and trafficking in child pornography, marital rape, and stalking. The connection of these issues to sexual harassment is twofold: one, the infraction is of a sexual nature; and, two, the victims are controlled, either physically or through coercion, by a power-seeking manipulator. In all, the public seeks to understand what motivates the perpetrator of such crimes and abuses and how we can protect ourselves from being victims.

Sexual harassment in middle or junior high schools and in high schools is either non-existent or rampant, depending upon whom you talk to. Generally, the higher up the administrative ladder in a school you go, the more denial you encounter that a problem exists. At the bottom of the ladder are the victims, the students--both boys and girls--who must endure the daily taunts and physical invasions of their bodies. Fortunately, more teachers and administrators are acknowledging that sexual harassment is a problem in their schools. Some schools now have curricula in place that teach students not only what sexual harassment is but also what students can do about it. They have in-service programs to educate all their employees about this form of harassment. And they are working to help eliminate it from their schools. For those schools that have no policy on sexual harassment, it is imperative they develop one, and it is to them that this book is directed.

This book can help a teacher or administrator avoid liability for sexual harassment, or, in the current jargon, it can effect "risk minimization." The book offers a legal definition of sexual harassment, provides examples of sexually harassing behavior, and explains the applicable laws. It deals with various relationships within the school setting in which sexual harassment may be encountered. Harassment can occur in the employment setting: between administrators and teachers, administrators and other school personnel, independent contractors and school personnel, supervisors and teachers, and teachers and teachers. It can also occur outside the employment context: between teachers and students, students and students, between students and other employees, such as bus drivers, or between students and non-employees, such as repair workers. It is also possible to have third-party sexual harassment claims by a person who was "injured" but who is not directly either the perpetrator or the victim.

The book begins with an explanation of sexual harassment and ends with suggestions for preventing it as well as strategies for handling incidents of harassing behavior. Part 1 defines the subject matter--What is sexual harassment? It emphasizes that men and women may perceive the same behavior in different ways, discusses the effects of sexual harassment, and suggests appropriate behavior in the school setting. Part 2, the heart of the book, explains the laws applicable to sexual harassment-- federal, civil, and criminal--and the liability that schools and individuals may incur for disregarding the laws. Part 3 discusses preventive measures schools are obligated to take in order to comply with federal laws as well as other measures they may choose to take to prevent sexual harassment. Part 4 offers suggestions on how to deal with incidents of sexually harassing behavior and lists steps schools can take to prevent recurrence. Finally, the Appendixes provide information about additional resources as well as the names and addresses of state and federal agencies that deal with sex discrimination. Within the text, a number of forms and questionnaires are included to help a school assess the extent of any problems with sexual harassment and to facilitate reporting by students or employees of incidents of harassment.

Ultimately, avoidance of liability is not the best reason to put a stop to harassment. The best reason is that ending harassment enables all students to pursue their educations more freely, to cooperate and learn from each other, and to contribute to their schools and community. Once it is stopped, teachers and administrators are better able to see their pupils individually rather than stereotypically. Putting an end to sexual harassment enhances the morale of the entire school and the confidence and self-respect of its individual students and school personnel.

1
What Is Sexual Harassment?

Simply put, sexual harassment is unwelcome sexual behavior. The behavior can take the form of sexual jokes, pictures, comments (verbal or written), name-calling, gossip, ogling, pinching, leering, gesturing, touching, brushing up against, blocking movement, threatening sexual assault, or actual sexual assault.

That definition, broad as it is, encompasses many of the actions prohibited by Title VII of the Civil Rights Act of 1964. That Act attempted to remedy discrimination in several areas, among them public accommodations and federally-assisted programs. Title VII of the Act protects workers from sex discrimination in employment. Not until 1980 did the Equal Employment Opportunity Commission (EEOC), in its "Guidelines on Discrimination," define sexual harassment as a form of unlawful, sex-based discrimination. Expanded in 1984 to include educational institutions, the Guidelines now state,

Unwelcome sexual advances, requests for sexual favors, and other verbal or physical conduct of a sexual nature constitutes sexual harassment when 1) submission to such conduct is made either explicitly or implicitly a term or condition of an individual's employment or academic advancement, 2) submission to or rejection of such conduct by an individual is used as the basis for employment decisions or academic decisions affecting such individual, or 3) such conduct has the purpose or effect of unreasonably interfering with an individual's work or academic performance or creating an intimidating, hostile, or offensive working or academic environment.

The EEOC is charged with enforcing the Civil Rights Act. Its Guidelines, while not authoritative as law, have consistently been incorporated into court decisions and thus are often tantamount to law.

As Title VII prohibits sex discrimination in employment, Title IX of the Education Amendments of 1972 prohibits sex-based discrimination against either employees or students in educational institutions or programs that receive federal funds. It also requires those institutions to maintain grievance procedures in order to settle disputes quickly and equitably.

Title IX is enforced by the federal Office for Civil Rights (OCR) of the U.S. Department of Education. That Office defines sexual harassment as "verbal or physical conduct of a sexual nature, imposed on the basis of sex, by an employee or agent of a recipient that denies, limits, provides different, or conditions the provisions of, aid, benefits, services or treatment protected under Title IX." In addition, Title IX may be enforced by private litigation. This means that instead of, or in addition to, filing a complaint with OCR, a claimant may hire an attorney and bring suit against her school district in federal or state court. State statutes can also provide pupils and school personnel protection from sexual harassment (see, *e.g.*, Minn. Stat. Chapter 127.46, amended 1992, in the Appendix).

The following examples of sexually harassing behavior, compiled from the experiences of school attorneys, teachers, school administrators, and students, illustrate the types of behavior that come within the purview of the preceding definitions:

1. During class while students are working at their desks, the teacher walks around the class, "helping" students with their assignment. He stands next to the boys or leans over to help them. When he gets to the girls, he squats down beside them, lowers his voice, and pats them on the knee.
2. On the school bus a group of eighth grade boys single out a group of sixth graders for daily taunting. "Hey, you faggots getting any pussy?" "You still sleeping with your mama?" "Your sister is doing it with everyone."
3. During lunch two administrators, whose duties include patrolling the school building, habitually walk into a teachers' lounge. Acting as a comedy team, they tell sexist and "dirty" jokes, one administrator being the "straight man."
4. Before school, in a hall where a group of girls hang out every morning, the girls shout out comments to the boys as they walk past: "Hey, how 'bout those lips! I bet he knows what to do with them." "Now, isn't that a cute little butt. I'd like to see that in front of my face."
5. A secretary is cornered in the copying room by a teacher who is "overly friendly." He tells her, "I really like that dress. It shows off your figure." As she bends over to put more paper in the machine, he pats her on the rear end.
6. A guidance counselor shunts girls into classes traditionally taken by females, such as home economics. He dissuades them from taking upper-level science and mathematics classes. To a girl whose college application has been rejected he says, "Just find a rich husband."

How Pervasive Is Sexual Harassment Today?

In the Workplace--Surveys by the U.S. Merit Systems Protection Board in 1981 and in 1988 of sexual harassment in the government found that 42% of the women and 14-15% of the men questioned had experienced sexual harassment.

In *Redbook's* survey of 9,000 working women published in November, 1976, almost 90% of them reported having experienced sexual harassment at work.

Among blue-collar workers, a survey revealed that 36% of the women and 18% of the men reported that they had been harassed.[3]

The Equal Employment Opportunity Commission (EEOC), the agency that enforces employment-discrimination laws, reports that sexual harassment charges filed in the first half of the 1992 fiscal year have increased by more that 50%, to 4,754 complaints from 3,135 in the same reporting period the year before. During the last fiscal year, the EEOC received 70,000 complaints, the greatest number in the history of the Commission.

In the Military--A 1990 Pentagon study of 20,000 personnel in the military reported that 64% of the women surveyed said they had been sexually harassed. Seventeen percent of men surveyed reported that they had been harassed by a male or female colleague.[4]

In a Navy study of 6,700 personnel, 75% of the women and 50% of the men said harassment had occurred within their commands.[5]

On College Campuses--Surveys repeatedly support the statistic that 20 - 30% of college women have been sexually harassed by male faculty during their college years.[6]

A survey of Cornell University women students found that 78% of those responding had experienced sexist comments and 68% had received unwelcome attention from their male peers.[7]

In a study at the Massachusetts Institute of Technology, 92% of the women and 57% of the men had experienced at least one form of unwanted sexual attention and had reacted negatively to it.[8]

In High Schools--A 1993 Harris poll of 1,632 students in grade 8-11, commissed by the AAUW, found that 85% of girls and 76% of boys said they had been sexually harassed in school.

Research results from a 1981 survey of high school students in Massachusetts revealed that sexual harassment is a problem in both comprehensive and vocational high schools.[9] That same study indicated that teacher-to-student sexual harassment is less prevalent than student-to-student harassment.

The March, 1988 issue of the *National Association of Secondary Schools Bulletin* carried the results of a 1986 survey of male and female juniors and seniors, ages 16 to 18, enrolled in a Minnesota secondary vocational center. That study showed that 33% to 60% of the 133 females responding reported experiencing some form of sexual harassment; only 1 of the 130 males questioned said he had been the victim of sexual harassment.

A study reported by the American Association of University Women in *How Schools Shortchange Girls* found that 65% of female high school students in nontraditional courses reported harassment by male classmates and by some teachers.[10]

Especially vulnerable among students are those who

1. enter non-traditional fields where they are perceived as "barging into" an area where they "don't belong" and where they will later be competing with members of the opposite sex for jobs.
2. are nearer in age to the age of their teachers.
3. are a member of a minority group and are harassed as a form of racism or because of stereotypes.
4. are inexperienced, unassertive or socially isolated, leaving them vulnerable to an exploitative relationship.

Further statistical information compiled by the Office of Equal Opportunity and Affirmative Action at the University of Minnesota in 1991 reveals that:

--Sexual harassment is *primarily* a problem for women, with more that 95% of reported cases occurring when a male of greater power harasses a female of lesser power. About 3-4% are cases of men harassing other men.
--One estimate states that only 5% of all men are harassers; the extent of harassment by females is unknown.
--Sexual harassment affects women of all kinds: all races, all ages, all occupations, all classes.
--Miscommunication based on stereotypes about race or culture contributes to problems with sexual harassment.
--Reports of sexual harassment are almost never false, or made out of a desire to harm or embarrass someone. In fact, in a majority of cases the harasser verifies the account of what happened. Failure to report is a much greater problem, complicating institutional efforts to end harassment.

If national and state statistics are unpersuasive regarding the prevalence of sexual harassment, administrators can determine whether sexual harassment exists in their schools simply by asking their students. Inquiries may be initiated with an overall school survey. The survey form in Part 3 of this book can be adapted to the particular needs of a school. It is important that the term sexual harassment is defined for students before they respond to a survey and that the survey be conducted with seriousness. After the survey is administered and the results tabulated, if sexual harassment is indicated, other, less formal follow-up methods of uncovering sexual harassment may be used. Informal small-group discussions in classes or in sessions conducted by guidance counselors may be helpful.

It may also be useful to survey administrators, faculty, and other staff members to determine whether they perceive a problem with sexual harassment in school (see Part 3). The survey should include not only questions about adult observations of students harassing students but also questions about adult observations of adults being harassed by school personnel and students being harassed by school personnel. Tabulating responses by gender can be instructive.

Faced with sexual harassment problems among employees, business corporations find that the programs that most successfully put an end to harassment are those in which corporate leadership is strong and decisive. The same principle applies in schools. The chief administrators set an example by regarding sexual harassment as a critical problem, one for which there will be zero-tolerance. Without leadership from top school personnel who confront the problem head-on, sexual harassment will remain a problem.

Myths and Misconceptions

In 1979, the Alliance Against Sexual Coercion (AASC) compiled a list of erroneous assumptions people make about sexual harassment. The list below is adapted from the AASC's compilation. These myths perpetuate sexual harassment, contribute to the victim's feelings of guilt, and induce women to keep quiet about sexual harassment. Although few people believe all these myths, there is sufficient misinformation about sexual harassment to warrant exposure of the facts that contradict the myths. Many of the assumptions below apply to men as well as to women.

> *Myth*: If women don't speak up about sexual harassment, then it's not happening.
> *Reality*: Women don't report sexual harassment because they feel isolated, guilty, scared of losing their jobs.
> *Reality*: We can begin to eliminate sexual harassment at the workplace only when we share and understand our experiences. If we remain silent, workplace harassment will continue to be seen as a personal problem rather than as

a social issue. These two myths will operate until so many women speak up about sexual harassment that our society can no longer pretend it doesn't happen.

Myth: Women invite sexual harassment by their behavior and/or dress.

Reality: As with rape, sexual harassment is not a sexually motivated act. It is an assertion of hostility and/or power expressed in a sexual manner. Sexual harassment is not in any way the fault of the woman.

Reality: Often women are expected to act or dress seductively both to get and keep their jobs.

Myth: Only women in certain occupations are likely to be sexually harassed.

Reality: Waitresses, flight attendants, and secretaries are not the only victims of sexual harassment. Women who work in factories, at professional jobs, and all kinds of jobs, consistently report this problem. Students, clients of professionals (doctors, dentists, therapists, etc.), domestic workers and babysitters also suffer sexual harassment and abuse.

Myth: Black women are exposed to sexual activity at an early age, are more sensuous and are not as upset by harassment.

Myth: Asian women are more submissive than other women and would be less likely to be offended by sexual harassment.

Reality: These are patently racist assumptions and constitute another example of blaming the victim rather than the harasser.

Myth: It is harmless to harass women verbally or to pinch or pat them. Women who object have no sense of humor.

Reality: Harassment is humiliating and degrading. It under-mines women's school or work performance and often threatens their education or economic livelihood. Women victimized by sexual harassment suffer emotionally and physically. Women should not be prepared to endure degradation with a smile.

Myth: A firm "no" is enough to discourage any man's sexual advances.

Reality: Because people believe women say no when they really mean yes, men often dismiss women's resistance. Men's greater physical, economic, and social power en-ables them to override the firmest "no." It should not be women's responsibility to ensure that sexual harassment doesn't happen.

Myth: Women who remain in a job where they are sexually harassed are masochistic or are really enjoying it.

Reality: Women's lower socio-economic position in the U.S. means that many are unable to quit their jobs or find new employment.

Myth: Only bosses are in a position to harass women at the workplace.

Reality: Co-workers and clients can also harass women at the workplace. Clients threaten to withdraw their busi-ness. Co-workers make work intolerable. Both complain to the boss, or already have the boss's support.

Myth: If women can't handle the pressure of the working world, they should stay home.

Reality: Women work out of economic necessity. Staying home is not an option for most working women. Nor, as we know from current publicity on wife abuse, is staying home a protection against sexual harassment.

Myth: Women make false charges of sexual harassment.

Reality: Women who speak out against sexual harassment meet with negative reactions, ranging from disbelief and ridicule to loss of job. Women have little to gain from false charges.

Myth: Women sleep their way to "the top" and other positions of power.

Reality: Very few women hold positions of power. For those isolated cases where women have tried to engage in sexual activity to gain promotions, evidence shows that it ultimately works against their advancement. This myth works against a woman who gives in to sexual pressure because she is then mistrusted by fellow workers.

Myth: Only certain men harass women at work.

Reality: All types of men, in all occupations, whether or not they hold positions of power, have been reported as harassers.

Myth: There are adequate procedures to take care of men who seriously assault or threaten women at work.

Reality: Society continues to view sexual harassment from a double standard. While the sexual harassers are tolerated, boys will be boys, the women victims bear the brunt of the blame. Personnel managers, union representatives, human right agencies, courts, and legislators reflect these discriminatory attitudes. Women who seek assistance from these sources to stop sexual harassment are frequently placing themselves at risk of humiliating indifference, ridicule, or even further sexual insinuation and harassment. Nevertheless, it is important to use these channels where possible.

Additionally, many men--and some women--wonder what all the fuss is about. They believe that if Anita Hill hadn't caused such a stir and if the media hadn't responded with enthusiasm by publishing thousands of articles about sexual harassment, we wouldn't be hearing much about it today. As these people see it, the issue of sexual harassment has gotten out of hand. As a result, what may have been an occasional, minor problem is now an issue of exaggerated proportions. High school administrators who admit they have problems in their schools with drugs and weapons may steadily deny that a problem with sexual harassment exists. Some administrators believe that educating students about sexual harassment is comparable to educating them about sex: if you teach them about the subject, they will just go out and do it more. Or they may believe that if you tell students about sexual harassment, you will encourage students to complain about it. (That is true.) They believe that education will encourage false reporting of harassment. Even if they do admit that a sexual harassment problem exists in their school, some administrators don't want to confront it. They believe they have enough problems during the average school day dealing with disgruntled parents, weapons on campus, precocious sexual behavior, racial disturbances, teachers' unions, and reduced budgets.

By refusing to deal with sexual harassment, administrators not only increase their own liability, they also forego the opportunity to remedy a problem that deprives girls of an equal education with boys. Sexually harassing behavior does not begin after high school graduation. It starts in elementary school, and the foundations for the behavior are laid in the homes and society in which we live.

Why Would Anyone Do That?
Why would a boy seated in back of a girl in a classroom repeatedly attempt to snap the girl's brastrap? Why would a male teacher fondle a female student when she is standing next to him to ask him a question about her history lesson? Why would a student scrawl obscene remarks about another student on the walls of a restroom?

To a casual observer, these behaviors may seem sexually motivated. Most psychologists and counselors believe, however, that the behaviors are motivated more by a desire for power than for sex. Males who sexually harass women see the role of the male as that of the aggressor, the one who makes the first moves in approaching women, and the one who controls the relationship. In the current jargon, these men "objectify" women; that is, they treat women as objects rather than as fellow human beings. They attach great significance to a woman's physical attributes and have little consideration for her character, her personality, her talents, and her intelligence. In short, they do not regard women as their equals, and they show it by their lack of respect for women in general. They believe that, although women may protest or feign coyness, they enjoy their advances. They also argue that women who say "no" don't really mean it-- they are pleased by being touched or complimented by men. As one high school boy, who was both intelligent and handsome stated, "Why would a girl not be flattered if I went up to her and put my arm around her? I'm just showing that I like her, that she's popular."

A Matter of Perception

Part of the difficulty with recognizing sexual harassment is that men and women do not always perceive behavior in the same way. A 1980-81 telephone survey of 1,200 Los Angeles residents conducted by Dr. Barbara Gutek of the University of Arizona Business School is instructive. Sixty-seven percent of the men surveyed said they would be complimented if propositioned by a female co-worker; only 17% of the women said a workplace proposition would be a compliment. In the same survey, 63% of the women but only 15% of the men said they would be insulted by it. In another study reported in *Harvard Business Review*, March-April 1981, male and female workers responded to the behavior of a co-worker who suggestively eyed female workers up and down. While only 8% of the men characterized the behavior as harassment, 24% of the women did.

The November 1992 issue of *American Bar Association Journal* reported the results of a two-year study of male and female lawyers in the federal courts of nine Western states.[11] Among the findings were that 29% of the women lawyers said they had seen male attorneys single out female non-lawyers for demeaning treatment. Only 8% of the male lawyers said they had witnessed such behavior. Additionally, more than 33% of the women lawyers said they had seen judges cut off presentations by female lawyers or address them less professionally than they do men. Only 6% of the male lawyers recalled seeing a judge cut off a female lawyer. And only 10% of the male lawyers said they had observed a judge addressing a woman colleague unprofessionally. As Lynn Hecht Schafran, director of the NOW Legal Defense and Education fund stated, "Women have different experiences and perceptions than men. And men either aren't there when it's [sexual harassment] happening or don't see it for what it is." The irony is that the federal courts in the Western part of the country where this survey was conducted are generally regarded as leaders in advancing the rights of women in the workplace.

The Development of Male/Female Roles

A major factor that accounts for these differences in perception is that boys and girls are not reared the same way. Within the same family, they are treated differently. Traditionally, a girl is more protected. Her whereabouts are more vigilantly monitored, her friends more carefully screened. She is expected to be more "domestic" than her brother, to learn to cook and to clean up and to be neat. She is taught to be "nice," to be accommodating, not to make a scene by speaking her mind or speaking too loudly. Her brother's unruly behavior is often excused with a "Boys will be boys" explanation; he is more readily forgiven for sowing a few wild oats. Girls are encouraged to pursue safe, feminine activities: dancing lessons, cheerleading, "candy-striping" at a local hospital. Boys are encouraged to play rough sports, to be aggressive, to take risks, and not to cry.

Elizabeth Grauerholz and Mary A. Koralewski analyze the way these roles are extended in school:[12] In middle school and high school, extracurricular activities continue to structure the social world of teenagers. Male athletic activities are the main cultural events of secondary schools, providing male athletes with considerable status among their peers. The importance of athletics for peer status is underscored by the structural and financial support male athletic programs receive, especially in comparison to girls' athletics, boys' minor sports, music, drama, art, and academic clubs. The implicit message to students is that males are to be supported and cheered on in their athletic activities, particularly in sports such as football and basketball, and females are to be supportive and decorative, despite women's increased participation in active roles like sports.

The results of the disparate expectations for boys and for girls is that an inordinate amount of emphasis is placed on girls to be physically attractive and socially adept. Yet the rules of behavior are not finely delineated. Although girls are expected to attract males, it is unclear how far this attraction is supposed to go. As a result, Grauerholz continues, "Women learn to be coy, manipulative, and subtle in social interaction rather than learning how to identify and directly state their desires and needs.[13]

Boys are rewarded for a narrow range of primarily athletic achievement, reinforcing the male "macho" stereotype. "Sexual activity becomes a means for achieving and proving one's masculinity to both self and peers, particularly since the number of males who can acquire status through athletics is limited."[14] The result is that many males feel pressured into sexual activity before they are ready.

Separate gender roles, encouraged at home and at school, affect the curriculum choices girls make and the responses boys make to those choices. In a chapter on sexual harassment in the book *Sexuality and the Curriculum*[15], the authors point to the reluctance of female students to enter non-traditional classes, programs, and occupations, such as mathematics, science, and technology. "When trailblazing females do enter these classes, they are often harassed for having greater opportunities to 'move up' and act unfemale; male students often resent the competition for their 'rightly deserved' space and feel pushed down to positions of less power. . . .Sexual harassment is thus used as a convenient mechanism for keeping women down 'in their place' and blocking their chances for economic opportunity and self-sufficiency."[16]

In addition to affecting the curriculum choices girls make, the establishment of separate gender roles also affects how males and females respond to sexual harassment. Research by Inger W. Jensen and Barbara A. Gutek[17] shows that men, in general, are more likely than women to blame girls for being sexually harassed. If a woman adheres to traditional sex roles, she will be likely to blame other women as well as herself for incidents of sexual harassment. She will also be more likely to relate the incident to friends, rather than to report it to someone in authority.

The media exacerbates these traditional boy/girl roles by ubiquitously portraying women as sexual objects, whether in a situation comedy, a music video or a television commercial. Women are displayed as young, attractive, sexy, sweet-smelling "babes." Those girls not fitting into this stereotypical category are mocked or are not depicted at all. Men, on the other hand, are portrayed as having a constant biological, sexual drive that is always in need of satisfaction. The right to have this drive met, even though it requires coercion, is implied by the media. Grauerholz claims that women feel responsible for men's pleasure and therefore have a difficult time saying "no." In general, she writes, "[Y]oung women emerge from adolescence ill equipped to respond clearly and assertively to the demands of males."[18]

As girls grow older, they perceive themselves subject to a different set of dangers than boys do. Fear of obscene telephone calls, leering looks, and sexual assaults are common fears of most women as well as girls. These are rational fears. According to the 1992 Uniform Crime Reports compiled by the Department of Justice, in 1991 a forcible rape occurred in the United States every four minutes and nine seconds, an increase of almost 4% from the preceding year. A June 1992 report from Surgeon General Antonia Novello states that violence is the leading cause of injury to women age 15-44. Sexual harassment creates apprehension that much greater harm will follow. If a man on a subway ogles a woman and makes suggestive mo-tions with his tongue, if a supervisor blocks a secretary's way to the water cooler, if a male student follows a female down the hall whispering obscenities to her, the victim is apprehensive that further forms of attack will follow. Girls fear these "little rapes" are only a prelude to an outright physical sexual assault.

Many males who harass never see their own behavior as threatening to others. They may think they are teasing when they pin a girl up against a locker at school. Or they may think that because a joke or sexual comment is not directed specifical-ly at an individual woman in a group, women will not find the joke offensive. They assume that because a woman does not complain about a man's dirty jokes, or even laughs, that she enjoys them. A fact sheet compiled by the University of Minne-sota in 1991 states that what many women see as threatening, offensive, humiliating or inappropriate, many men see as flat-tering or friendly behavior. In the words of these women, exas-perated by the failure of men to comprehend the anguish of sexual harassment described by Anita Hill during the Clarence Thomas Supreme Court confirmation hearings, "They [men] just don't get it."

While there is pressure to conform to traditional boy/girl roles, girls are becoming more aware that they have other op-tions than to conform. Girls and women in the eighties and nineties have increasingly been encouraged--at home and at school--to speak out, to believe that only they have the right to control their own bodies, and to protest sexual harassment.

The changing roles of men and women contribute to the confusion regarding sexual harassment. More women are taking on jobs traditionally held by men. Fifty percent of medical school and law school students are women. Women are entering trades, such as welding, because they can make more money than they can in a pink collar job. The increase in the number of women in the workforce as a whole causes many men to feel uncomfortable and uncertain whether "new rules" of behavior now apply both on and off the job. Those men who feel threatened by a female "invasion" of their jobs, their clubs, and their recreational facilities instinctively want to maintain their status and power. They do that by attempting to exert power over women--through their language and their behavior. A pinch or a pat or an off-color comment reassures them that they are in control of the situation and that they have the upper hand.

Although the term "sexual harassment" was not used until the mid-seventies, the form of abuse is not new. However, the difference between today and twenty-five years ago is that girls and women now have a legal claim against sexual harassment and the potential for a remedy in the form of injunctive relief, reinstatement of their jobs, back pay and other monetary damages. Due to the heightened awareness that they have the right to reject sexual advances, women are more frequently protesting sexual harassment at school and on the job by taking their cases to court. Yet, even with the support of numerous laws and employers' firm policies against sexual harassment, many girls and women, perhaps most, do not complain to people who are in a position to do something about the harassment. If they were truly being abused, wouldn't they tell someone?

Why Don't Women Tell?

A sampling of reasons given by girls for not reporting sexual harassment:

--I told the teacher, but she said, "I didn't see it; there's nothing I can do about it. Go sit down."
--I was afraid no one would believe me.

--I thought it might make his behavior worse, that he would tell all his friends and they would gang up on me.
--I figured if I just ignored it, the harassment would stop.
--Who would I tell?
--I thought it was somehow my fault, that there must be something I was doing to cause it to happen.
--He threatened to "get me" if I told.
--I didn't know how to describe what was happening.
--I was too embarrassed to tell.
--I doubted the school would or could do anything about it.
--My parents would kill me.

Peer harassment in schools is far more prevalent than teacher-student harassment. In fact, harassment is so common in our schools that girls often feel that it is just another part of the school day, like fifth-period algebra. Complaints are generally treated with indifference by teachers and school administrators. One girl stated, "People tell me to forget it--that it's just high school and that I shouldn't feel bothered. But what about later on? Will people say, 'Oh, it's just the office, don't get so upset?'" [19] Will they also say, "That's just the Navy or the factory or the legislature" if the harassment continues after high school?

Boys are likely to sexually harass girls in groups. Most faculty members have witnessed the following scenario so often, they no longer notice it. This scene could occur in most any high school in the United States: boys line the school corridors and sit in groups in the cafeteria. They participate in "scoping." They yell out to the girls who pass and discuss their physical attributes. Or they rate the girls, using numbers from 1 to 10, shouting out, "She's a five!" They call unattractive girls "dogs" and bark at them. One boy wears a tee shirt saying, "No fat chicks." The shirt bears a picture of an overweight girl overlaid with a red circle diagonally slashed. Another boy refers to a girls' breasts as "jugs" or "melons." Harassment during teen years occurs at a time when girls are most vulnerable, when many are extremely self-conscious about their bodies.

Some teachers and administrators are responsive to the girls' complaints of peer harassment. Others aren't aware there's even a problem or, if they do perceive a problem, consider it a personal matter between the boy and the girl. One principal claimed that what may look like harassment is often just "harmless adolescent exploration." Boys who harass may admit to the behavior, for example, lifting a girl's skirt, but deny that it's sexual harassment. To them, it may just be a joke.

Sexual harassment by a teacher, while less common than harassment by a peer, does happen. In its subtler forms, girls may be unable to articulate what is going on. They may claim that a teacher makes them feel "uncomfortable." When pressed for details they may say the teacher stares at their faces or their bodies. He may get too close when he talks to them. Or he may touch their hair or their faces. Often several girls will make the same complaint. Due to their inexperience, the girls may have a feeling that something is wrong, but they may be reluctant to tell anyone because they can't specifically explain the source of their uneasiness.

The effect in the classroom is that the girls who are harassed are not full participants in the class. They may be reluctant to speak up or to ask questions. They may try to remain as anonymous as possible. Often they fear their grades will suffer if they are unresponsive to the teacher or that he will refuse to give them a good recommendation for a job or to get into college. In many cases, they drop the class so they won't have to contend with the harassment.

The feelings and experiences of sexually harassed adult women are similar to those expressed by high school girls. Women, as well as girls, under-report sexual harassment. Formal complaints or legal assistance is sought by only 1 to 7% of harassed women.[20] That figure is corroborated by the 1988 U.S. Merit Systems Protection Board survey which showed that only 5% of harassed government employees actually filed formal complaints or requested investigations.

Fear of retaliation was the main reason given by respondents to a 1988 survey by *Working Woman* for not reporting incidents of harassment. Many women delayed reporting because they mistrusted the complaint structure; they feared lack of confidentiality in the grievance procedure. Some women even quit their jobs rather than complain. One teenager employed in a department store, who was frequently harassed by her boss in the stockroom, left her job and found another without telling her parents why she quit. "They wouldn't have let me work anywhere anymore," she said, "and I needed the money."

Other women report they are too embarrassed or they don't want to be labeled "trouble-makers" or bad sports. It may be too painful to confront the grievance official if he is the same sex as the harasser or too awkward if he is a close friend of the harasser. Some women think they should be able to handle the harasser on their own without seeking help from a supervisor. Still others think having to put up with unwanted sexual advances is part of the job and must be endured along with the whistles and cat-calls of construction workers. Being socialized to be nice and accommodating also helps to explain why women don't complain; they have been conditioned not to cause trouble. Fear of losing their jobs is another major reason women may not report sexual harassment. Most women who work need the money and don't have the option of being out of work until they find another job. In addition, investigations into allegations of harassment may be lengthy and embarrassing. Taking legal action is expensive and slow.

Even if women don't follow the company grievance procedure to report sexual harassment, they may tell a close friend at work about the harassment. In some cases the harassment is so conspicuous that numerous women already know about it. Yet, it is not uncommon for a conspiracy of silence to occur among women who have been harassed. Women develop coping skills to dodge the company "groper." In one corporation, a supervisor called female employees singly into his office and fondled himself while he talked to them. The supervisor became more red-faced and short of breath as he spoke. The women in the office code-named him "Fingers" and invented reasons to stay out of his office or at least to keep the door open when they were inside. But no woman in the office complained to anyone in authority about the behavior, which persisted until the supervisor retired. The incident points up another aspect of harassers: they often repeat the same pattern of behavior on successive victims. They may use the same approach and even the same words with each new woman harassed.

Although most large corporations now have formal anti-discrimination policies and procedures to follow in order to make a complaint, schools have been slow to comply with EEOC guidelines and Title IX regulations. Not only are many school employee handbooks and student handbooks without a policy against sexual harassment, they also have no specific grievance procedure to follow to lodge a harassment complaint. In one southern high school the only way for an employee to file a grievance of any kind was to write a formal letter to the district superintendent of education with a copy to the principal of the school in which the employee worked. Under those conditions, it is not surprising that few complaints were filed.

What Are the effects of Sexual Harassment?

"Peer Harassment: Hassles for Women on Campus," a publication of the Project on the Status and Education of Women, summarizes the impact of peer harassment: "Peer harassment, like faculty harassment, sends the message that a woman is not equal to a man. She is an object of scorn or derision. She is not being taken seriously as a person; she is not valued."[21] The message can "weaken a woman's self-esteem or self-confidence and can undermine her academic, vocational, and personal goals."[22] "The psychological symptoms and effects of sexual harassment may include anger, fear, depression, anxiety, irritability. . .feelings of humiliation, embarrassment, shame and alienation, and a sense of helplessness and vulnerability."[23] Not taking any action to halt the harassment makes a victim feel worse. As a girl from West Oakland, California, wrote, "[I]t makes me feel like a coward and reminds me how I'm not really doing anything to help solve the problem, which makes me feel bad about myself."

A recent article by Adrian LeBlanc in *Seventeen* magazine described the way sexual harassment impacts on girls: "The presence of harassment changes your way of being in the world, the way you do things, where you get to do them, and what you'd like to do."[24] Girls may switch a class or even a major to avoid the harassment. LeBlanc adds, "Your options shrink--you don't feel like playing soccer because of what the guys yell at the girls on the field."

Nan Stein, Project Director of a research project on sexual harassment and abuse in elementary and secondary schools, states that students who experience even subtle forms of sexual harassment may feel "less trusting of people in general, and less enthusiastic about pursuing their education. Victims/subjects of sexual harassment, as well as the bystanders and witnesses to such incidents, express a loss of confidence in the effectiveness of school policies."[25] Tolerance of sexual harassment may jeopardize students' positive feelings about justice and caring in their society.

Sexual harassment can also cause physical problems: headaches, stomach aches, insomnia, loss of appetite, weight loss, and crying spells. It interferes with a student's ability to do her school work and increases the likelihood of absence from school. Sexual harassment makes life unpleasant in the classroom and at the office. An employee who refuses to give in to the sexual demands of her supervisor risks losing her job or a promotion. Cumulatively, it discourages women from asserting themselves in the workplace and can lead them to quit their jobs. Over 20% of women have quit a job, been transferred, been fired, or quit trying to get a job because of harassment.[26]

Males also suffer when they sexually harass women. If they harass with impunity, it makes such behavior seem acceptable. It may also be difficult for a man who persistently harasses women to develop healthy relationships with them since he has so little respect for women. Overall, men who sexually harass women have a hard time relating to women as human beings, which also contributes to trouble in the workplace where many of their co-workers are women.[27]

Sexual harassment is expensive. The 1988 *Working Woman* study found that sexual harassment costs the typical Fortune 500 company $6.7 million a year in increased absenteeism, employee turnover, low morale and low productivity. Studies by the U.S. Merit Systems Protection Board show that harassment of federal government workers cost the government $267 million in two years due to lost productivity and employee turnover. More recently, in Minnesota, failure of the Duluth school district to erase the obscenities written about a female student on the stalls of the boys' bathroom at Central High resulted in a settlement that cost the district $15,000. In February, 1992, the United States Supreme Court held that monetary damages can now be awarded in a Title IX discrimination suit. The potential for individual and school district liability is great.

In addition to being costly, sexual harassment suits cause resentment in the community. Where dollars must be stretched to cover academic needs, taxpayers resent having their taxes spent on lawsuits and settlements that could have been avoided. Parents also become concerned about the quality of their children's education and the dangers of the environment in which their children must learn. Diminished community support for the schools is detrimental to both school employees and to the children the schools are attempting to educate.

How Is a Person Supposed to Act?

Confusion prevails about whether a new set of rules or a new code of conduct has been instituted in the workplace as a result of potential liability for sexual harassment. Men are puzzled about the rules of proper conduct. They ask, "Can I say she looks good in that sweater?"

Those who doubt that a true sexual harassment problem exists accuse women who argue that a problem does exist with either misrepresenting what is, in effect, a personal attraction between two people or of trying to improve the manners of a few boorish men. From one perspective, no rules have changed; respectful people have always been considerate of and sensitive to the wishes and feelings of others. From another perspective, it is advisable to be circumspect and to assess one's own attitudes and behaviors. Regardless of the intent of the speaker, the behavior he regards as harmless may be considered offensive by the person on the receiving end.

Teachers and administrators need to see that besides functioning as educators, they also serve as role models to their students. They should refrain from making reference to a student's physical appearance. Just as male faculty members do not usually comment on the bodies or clothing of their male students, they should not comment in a similar manner on the bodies of their female students. Remarking on a student's sex is as offensive as commenting on her race or religion. Discussions of a student's progress in a class should occur at school, during school hours, in an appropriate place. The same is true for a supervisor conferring with a co-worker or a subordinate. Telephone calls to the home, unless a teacher wishes to confer with a student's parents, are inappropriate. Asking questions that pry into a student's or employee's personal life is also out of bounds. In conversations, one should avoid comments that could have a sexual meaning. Giving personal birthday or holiday gifts is also improper at school.

Teachers and administrators should avoid physical contact with students and school personnel. Although a pat on the shoulder can help console a student or show that a teacher is pleased with her accomplishment, caresses that linger or touches that are too frequent should be avoided. Verbal comments that acknowledge that a job has been well done produce the same effect as a pat. An elementary school principal, who described himself as being from a demonstrative family, was in the habit of regularly hugging his students, both boys and girls. Not all the students wanted his hugs, and some felt uncomfortable at his touch. When a fifth-grade girl asked him not to hug her anymore, he was surprised and hurt. He told the girl's mother, "I never meant to offend her; I like all my students and I try to show them I care about them." In another case a teacher, who taught special education students in high school, was so pleased with a student's progress that she not only gave him a hug, but also an enthusiastic kiss on the cheek. The student was furious and complained to the principal and to his parents. The teacher was cautioned to show her enthusiasm in a less demonstrative way.

Finally, teachers and other school personnel should avoid gender-demeaning remarks and sexually oriented comments and jokes. A student supplied the following negative examples from her own school:[28]

--A student was constructing a sine curve at the blackboard and her teacher snickered, "Hey, everyone, doesn't Barbie have nice curves?"

--A history teacher announced that if the girls had a lower combined average on the history exam than the boys, they had to bake cakes for the guys, whereas in the reverse, the boys would have to buy something of the Sara Lee variety.

--An English teacher stated, "Only boys and intelligent girls will enjoy this book."

--Another teacher asked, "You don't have the homework ready? Oh, that's right--you girls do dishes every night."

It is important to keep in mind that the schools do not stand literally *in loco parentis*. The privileges of a parent to hug or to kiss a child are not those of a teacher or an administrator. Whether the preceding behaviors are harassment depends on whether they are welcomed by the recipient. Rather than guess whether a hug or a kiss is welcome, it is better to use restraint and not subject a student or adult to behavior he might consider offensive.

One means of determining whether one's behavior constitutes sexual harassment is to pose a series of questions. At a sexual harassment prevention workshop developed by the Minnesota Department of Education, participants were encouraged to ask themselves the following questions regarding their behavior:

1) Would I want my behavior to be the subject of a newspaper article or to appear on the evening news?
2) Is there equal power between me and the person I am interacting with?
3) Would I behave the same way if my wife, husband, parent, or significant other were standing right next to me?
4) Would I want someone else to act this way toward my wife, daughter, husband, son, parent or significant other?
5) Is there equal initiation and participation between me and the person I am interacting with?

The bottom line for teachers, administrators, and all school personnel is to treat males and females equally, to maintain a "hands-off policy," and to behave professionally toward school employees.

2
What Laws Apply to Schools and Individuals in the Area of Sexual Harassment?

Several federal statutes and numerous state laws apply to sexual harassment in the school setting. Both civil laws and criminal laws may apply. Two commonly invoked federal laws are Title VII of the 1964 Civil Rights Act (updated by the Civil Rights Act of 1991) and Title IX of the Education Amendments of 1972. Title VII applies to discrimination on the job, and Title IX applies to discrimination in those schools that receive federal funding (virtually all schools). Title VII prohibits discrimination based on race, color, religion, national origin, or sex; Title IX prohibits discrimination based on sex. Under Title VII and Title IX, sexual harassment is regarded as a form of sex discrimination. State laws may be similar to federal laws, and they may permit greater financial recovery as well as different types of recovery.

Under Title VII, a school district may be liable to its employees for the sexually harassing or otherwise discriminatory behavior of other school employees, such as supervisors and co-workers, and even of non-employees, such as independent contractors or consultants. Title VII is not available to students unless they are employed by the school. Thus, if a student is sexually harassed by a teacher or by another student, this statute will generally be inapplicable. However, students and other school employees, may have a cause of action under Title IX or under numerous state statutes. If a suit is brought for violation of state law, such as battery (intentional physical contact), the trial will be held in a state court, generally in the locale where the offense took place. If a suit is brought for violation of federal law, such as Title VII or Title IX, however, the case can wind up in a federal court, presided over by a federal judge, and with a jury composed of people who reside in the state but who may not be from the local area. The federal court may be miles from the site where the alleged offense occurred. Furthermore, if a case is predicated on both federal and state laws, it is possible that all claims will be handled in the federal court, including the state claims. The law that will be applied to the state claims is the law of the state in which the offense occurred.

Besides the location of the court, another difference between state and federal laws is that there can be different remedies, or penalties, if the offense is proved. For example, Title VII has a ceiling on the amount of *compensatory* and *punitive* damages that may be paid a claimant. (See Part 2, Remedies Under the Civil Rights Act of 1991 for further explanation of terms.) Depending on the number of employees in a school district, the maximum amount that can be awarded for compensatory and punitive damages is $50,000 to $300,000. Under state tort claims acts, a party may sue the state or local government for the torts of its employees who are acting within the scope of their employment. Claims against state or local governments brought under state tort claims acts also have a ceiling on monetary damages. Recovery under state tort law may be greater or lesser than that provided by federal law. Other state laws will permit a jury (or a judge, in a non-jury trial) to determine how much a claimant who wins her case should be paid. It is possible, therefore, for a claimant to be awarded thousands or even millions of dollars in a state civil suit.

In addition to federal and state civil laws, criminal law might also be applied to those who sexually harass others. A point to keep in mind is the difference between the criminal and the civil law. If a defendant is accused of committing criminal sexual conduct--rape, for example--that case is prosecuted by the state in the person of the district attorney (in a few states she may be called the solicitor). The standard of fault needed to get a conviction is "beyond a reasonable doubt." If there is any shred of a reasonable doubt in the jury's mind that the defendant is guilty, they must let the defendant go. If he is convicted, the penalty is usually imprisonment.

Civil cases, on the other hand, are not brought by the state, but by an individual or groups of individuals, the plaintiffs. If the plaintiff proves her case by a simple "preponderance of the evidence," meaning that the defendant can be even just slightly more at fault than not at fault (a simple negligence standard), the plaintiff will win her case. The jury need not be persuaded of the defendant's fault to the degree required by the criminal law. The penalty, or remedy, in a civil case is usually monetary damages and injunctive relief.

One further point is important for teachers and other school personnel to keep in mind. If a claimant brings suit under a state tort claims act, the employer usually assumes liability for its employee. In effect, the employee drops out of the suit. However, under state tort claims law, the school district will not defend that employee if the employee acted with malice or intent to harm or if he acted outside the scope of his employment.

School districts have their own attorneys, usually a firm kept on a retainer. That firm is paid to represent the school district. If a conflict of interest arises between the employee and the school district, it would be unethical for an attorney to represent both the employee and the school district. If it is discovered that the employee acted outside the scope of his employment or with intent to harm, the attorney will continue to represent the school district but will discontinue representing the employee in this matter. Each party would, therefore, have to have his own attorney. It is likely that the victim would sue both the school district and the teacher in the same lawsuit.

Even though sexual harassment suits receive a great deal of media attention, the majority of cases do not go to trial or involve lawyers. Most cases involving schools are resolved within the school district, either by agreement between the harasser and the person offended or by the district taking action to insure that the harassment has been ended. When suits are brought, however, litigation is time-consuming, slow, expensive, disruptive, and negative for the school district and its officials. The emotional costs for both the plaintiff and the defendant can be profound. The most desirable course of action is to prevent sexual harassment from occurring in the first place or to prevent liability on the part of the district if it does occur. A good way to begin is by studying the existing laws that cover discrimination and their attendant consequences.

Federal Law: The Civil Rights Act of 1964, Title VII

Title VII of the Civil Rights Act of 1964 makes it "an unlawful employment practice for an employer. . .to discriminate against any individual with respect to his compensation, terms, conditions, or privileges of employment, because of such individual's race, color, religion, sex, or national origin."
(42 U.S.C. sec. 2000e-2(a)(1))

The Act that prohibited discrimination in the workplace also created the Equal Employment Opportunity Commission (EEOC). The EEOC is a Commission established by Congress.

It issues important regulations and guidelines on discrimination, and in particular, sexual harassment. The guidelines define terms, explain EEOC policy, and provide examples to illustrate that policy.

It is important to note at the outset that if an employee brings a case against her employer under Title VII, she must first exhaust certain available administrative remedies. That is, she cannot bring a Title VII suit in court without going through the procedures outlined by the EEOC. The EEOC, usually acting through the state office in charge of civil rights, receives complaints based on discrimination and conducts investigations. It attempts to settle disputes between employers and their employees. It has the authority to go to court during an investigation and ask the court to take temporary action regarding an employee's work situation. It may issue subpoenas and force an employer to answer questions and to produce records.

Once the EEOC has investigated a case, it can either initiate a civil suit against the employer on its own, or, more likely, it can issue a "right-to-sue letter." The letter can be issued upon the occurrence of one of the following events: a) the claimant requests it, 180 days have elapsed since the employee filed a claim with the EEOC, and the EEOC investigation is incomplete; b) the EEOC has investigated and has made a determination of "no reasonable cause" in the case; or c) the EEOC has investigated and has determined the employee has cause to sue her employer, the EEOC has failed to achieve an agreement between the employer and the employee, and the EEOC has decided not to pursue the case itself. An employee should note that once the right-to-sue letter has been issued, should she decide to file a suit, she must file within 90 days from the day she receives the right-to-sue letter.

Although discrimination based on sex is mentioned in The Civil Rights Act of 1964, sexual harassment is not. That term did not come into common use until a decade later. The proviso against discrimination based on sex was attached to the bill at the last moment. Originally the Act only prohibited discrimination in employment based on race, color, religion, or national origin. Opponents of the bill thought it would surely be defeated if sexual equality were attached to it. Others believed sex discrimination was different from other types of discrimination and that separate legislation was needed to cover it. Because the Johnson administration wanted this bill passed, however, it did not oppose the amendment barring discrimination based on sex. Although discrimination based on sex was illegal after the passage of the bill and the Act was enforced, sexual harassment was not at first construed as violative of the Act.

In 1976, Judge Charles Richey, a federal judge in Washington, D.C., presided over a case in which a male supervisor retaliated against a female employee who had refused his sexual advances.[29] His decision was the first to specifically recognize sexual harassment as a form of sex discrimination. The court held that the behavior in question had only to create an "artificial barrier to employment that was placed before one gender and not the other, even though both genders were similarly situated." Conditions of employment that were applied differently to women than to men were sexual harassment, actionable under the Civil Rights Act of 1964 as sexual discrimination. Prior to that decision harassment had been characterized as a personal grievance by the woman employee against her harasser.

In 1980, the EEOC issued regulations defining sexual harassment and stating that it was a form of sex discrimination prohibited by the Civil Rights Act. The EEOC regulations and guidelines are not law, but they are very helpful to a court in explaining the ramifications of Title VII. Many of the guidelines have been incorporated into decisions of various courts. They were given significant weight in the landmark case of *Meritor Savings Bank v. Vinson*[30] in 1986.

Just as the guidelines are persuasive to courts, lower federal court decisions can be persuasive to higher courts. When decisions of lower federal courts are inconsistent in various parts of the country, the United States Supreme Court may choose to consider a case that is appealed in order to clarify the law. That is precisely what happened in the 1992 U.S. Supreme Court case of *Franklin v. Gwinnett County Public Schools*, when the Court held that a student who brought suit against her school under Title IX could be awarded monetary damages. Before that time, lower federal courts were split as to whether monetary damages could be awarded. The decisions of the Supreme Court become the law of the land and may not be ignored by any other state or federal court. But even the Supreme Court sometimes reverses itself. It is important to note, too, that rights guaranteed by the U.S. Constitution and interpreted by the Supreme Court represent "a floor, not a ceiling." That is, a state may legislate greater rights for its citizens than those given by the federal Constitution.

Types of Sexual Harassment Cases Under Title VII

Quid Pro Quo

Two types of sexual harassment cases have developed under Title VII: *quid pro quo* cases and hostile environment cases. Both types place the burden of proof on the complainant to prove that she was discriminated against on the basis of her sex --that is, had she been male, the discrimination would never have occurred.

Quid pro quo cases (literally, "that for this") were the earliest and may be the easiest to understand. An economic or other job benefit is conferred on a woman if she agrees to the sexual advances of her harasser, who is usually her supervisor; or she may be punished by that supervisor for failure to comply. EEOC guidelines divide *quid pro quo* harassment into two categories:

> Unwelcome sexual advances, requests for sexual favors, and other verbal or physical conduct of a sexual nature constitute sexual harassment when (1) submission to such conduct is made either explicitly or implicitly a term or condition of an individual's employment, [or] (2) submis-

sion to or rejection of such conduct by an individual is used as the basis for employment decisions affecting such individual. . . .
[*EEOC 1980 Guidelines on Sexual Harassment*, Sec. 1604.11(a) (1-2)].

In the early cases, plaintiffs asserted that they had been deprived of tangible job benefits because they rejected the sexual demands of their harasser. A plaintiff had to show a clear connection between the harassment and the job benefit of which she was deprived. If she could not, the harassment was considered a personal, isolated disagreement between the perpetrator and the employee, and the employee had no remedy.

To prove a *quid pro quo* case of sexual discrimination, the plaintiff must establish a number of elements. These elements were outlined in a 1982 case in the Florida district court, *Henson v. City of Dundee.*[31] In that case, a female dispatcher in the Dundee Police Department claimed that sexual harassment by the police chief led her to resign under duress. The criteria enumerated by the *Henson* court, and in other, related cases, to establish a *quid pro quo* case are summarized in a recent book, *Sexual Harassment in Employment Law.*[32] The complainant must show:

1) *Membership in a protected group.* The plaintiff may be either male or female, since the statute is designed to protect both sexes.
2) *Unwelcome sexual advances.* The usual form of advance is a direct sexual proposition that the subordinate must comply with in order to obtain or retain a tangible job benefit.
3) *An adverse employment action.* In a classic case a plaintiff must show that due to her rejection of her supervisor's advances, she was denied a promotion or a raise.
4) *The causal connection.* (a) that the sexual advance was because of the complainant's sex, and (b) that the complainant's reaction to the sexual advance affected a tangible aspect of the complainant's term, condition, or

privilege of employment. Here, the job detriment is not due to the plaintiff's gender but due to her refusal to comply with a sexual advance that was based on her gender. She must show a causal connection between her refusal and the loss of the job benefit.

5) *Employer responsibility*. This last, and most important, criterion established by the *Henson* court is that "an employer is strictly liable for the actions of its supervisors that amount to sexual discrimination or sexual harassment resulting in tangible job detriment to the subordinate employee." It does not matter whether the school district knew or should have known of the harassment: it will still be held liable. The significance of this last criterion is that a harasser with the power to grant or deny a subordinate's job benefit may provide the basis for the school district's liability under Title VII. Or, if a supervisor harasses the subordinate of another supervisor, he may still possess the authority to control the terms, conditions, or privileges of the complainant's employment through his relationship with the other supervisor. If the school principal determines whether a secretary is promoted or gets a pay raise, an assistant principal who harasses the secretary and is influential with the principal may still have his liability imputed to the school district. The *EEOC Policy Guide* (March 19, 1990) states that "[a]n employer will always be held responsible for acts of quid pro quo harassment." Even if a supervisor has no power to confer or deny a fellow employee a job benefit, if the employee is led to believe the supervisor will be influential in determining job enhancements, the employer may still be liable for the actions of the supervisor.

The unwelcomeness of sexual advances lies at the heart of any sexual harassment case, including *quid pro quo* harassment. In the *Henson* case the court defined unwelcome conduct as conduct that "the employee did not solicit or incite. . .[and] that the employee regarded. . .as undesirable or offensive." (p. 903). Unlike racial harassment, for example, which is always presumed unwelcome, sexual advances may be considered "romantic" or at least inoffensive. If the recipient is flattered or amused by the sexual overtures, then, of course, Title VII is not violated. An employee who uses foul language or sexual innuendo herself does not waive her legal protection from sexual harassment. However, because a plaintiff's behavior was "voluntary," that is, because she was not *forced* to have sexual relations against her will, does not mean that her behavior will provide a defense to the harasser under Title VII. The Supreme Court stated in *Meritor* that the "correct inquiry is whether respondent [Vinson] by her conduct, indicated that the alleged sexual advances were unwelcome, not whether her actual participation in sexual intercourse was voluntary." (p. 68). The main criterion used to determine if sexual harassment has occurred is whether the sexual conduct was unwelcome. And that can be a difficult fact to determine.

In some cases of harassment there may be witnesses who can confirm that the harasser made sexual advances or objectionable comments, or there may be additional corroborating evidence. But in other cases, the word of the alleged harasser will be pitted against that of the woman bringing suit against him. In these cases the credibility of the plaintiff or the defendant may be the decisive factor in determining who wins a case. When there is no corroborating evidence of welcomeness, the court will look at the totality of circumstances and regard each situation on a case-by-case basis. That includes the "nature of the sexual advances and the context in which the alleged incidents occurred." (*EEOC 1980 Guidelines on Sexual Harassment*, Sec. 1604.11(b)). In many cases, courts have looked at the provocativeness of the dress and language of the woman alleging she was harassed. There is no stated rule against the admissibility of this kind of testimony. The Supreme Court has advised the lower courts to "carefully weigh the applicable considerations in deciding whether to admit evidence of this kind." As a general rule, however, the sexual history of the woman will be considered irrelevant. More important factors to be considered are whether the recipient invited and encouraged the harasser's advances. Mere friendliness to the harasser is insufficient to prove welcomeness. Although reporting a grievance to the employer is not required in *quid pro quo* cases, it may be considered evidence of unwelcomeness.

Discrimination of the *quid pro quo* type may take unusual forms. For example, an employer may show favoritism toward an employee who submitted to his sexual advances or requests. Suppose an opening develops in a school for an assistant principal. The principal lets it be known to the female teachers that the teacher who can really be "nice" to him will get the job. A teacher who has been sexually coerced by the principal is promoted to that position. What of the other qualified employees who were not coerced? The *EEOC Policy Guide* (January 12, 1990) states that, "If a female employee is coerced into submitting to unwelcome sexual advances in return for a job benefit, other female employees who were qualified for but were denied the benefit may be able to establish that sex was generally made a condition for receiving the benefit." Naturally, if the reverse were true, and a male teacher were promoted to assistant principal after having been coerced into having sex with a female principal, other male teachers could claim *quid pro quo* discrimination. In the above example, the employer would also be liable to the coerced female employee for *quid pro quo* harassment.

Can a male teacher also avail himself of Title VII to protest the discriminatory promotion of a woman coerced by the principal into having sex with him? The guidelines say "yes." Third party suits by qualified employees, either male or female, who were denied a job benefit are foreseen by the EEOC. The qualified employees may challenge the favoritism displayed toward a coerced co-worker. "[I]n such a case, both women *and* men who were qualified for but who were denied the benefit can challenge the favoritism on the basis that they were injured as a result of the discrimination leveled against the woman who was coerced." *EEOC Policy Guide* (January 12, 1990).

One further issue needs to be considered: the burden of proof in a *quid pro quo* case. In a civil case, the person bringing the suit must convince the jury (or the judge, if the trial is non-jury) by a preponderance of the evidence that the defendant has committed the alleged wrong. In a *quid pro quo* case, this burden shifts to the defendant once the plaintiff has asserted the elements stated previously: The employee, as a member of a protected group was subjected to unwelcome sexual advances. As a result, there was an adverse employment action (for example, she was fired), and her refusal to comply with the sexual advances led to her firing. That is, once the plaintiff has shown that acquiescence to sexual advances was a condition of maintaining a job or getting a promotion, the employer then gets a chance to show there was a legal, non-discriminatory reason for the adverse employment decision. The employer will usually rebut the plaintiff's accusations by attempting to show there were no sexual advances made or, in the more likely scenario, that the advances were welcome. If the employer can show a legitimate reason for his treatment of the employee, for example, she had poor work performance, excessive absences or latenesses to work, or that she failed to follow school district policy, he can avoid liability. While not denying that the employee was sexually harassed, the employer must show that sexual harassment was not a causal link in the employment action taken (her quitting or being fired). The defendant may say, for example, that a teacher who claims sexual harassment really quit her job to take a different job closer to home.

The case does not end here. The burden of proof then shifts back to the plaintiff to show that the employer's reasons for the adverse job action, such as firing, were only pretextual. The plaintiff tries to offer evidence that establishes a connection between the harassment and the adverse action by the employer. She may attempt to show that prior to the adverse action her performance evaluations were high, that additional employees had to be hired to fill her position after she left, or that the school district failed to follow its own procedures in discharging her. If she has been accused of excessive absences, she may try to link the absences to the harassment. If she has "voluntarily" quit her job because she was harassed, she will need to show a causal connection between the sexual harassment and her decision to quit. The term for this type of quitting is "constructive discharge." The employee resigns because conditions at work are unbearable; in effect, her resignation is tantamount to being fired. These cases are difficult to prove; the decisive factor in the success of the argument may ultimately be the credibility of the witnesses each side offers.

In practice, many of the matters above are handled through "motions," that is, applications to the court or judge which are made in order to obtain a favorable ruling for the applicant. For example, a complainant may make a motion prior to trial to have certain evidence excluded. Successful motions narrow the focus of the trial, and in some cases, may entirely preclude a trial.

In cases of "mixed motive," where the employer acknowledges that even if the plaintiff has stated a case of sexual harassment that he would have made the same decision regarding the employee, he would formerly have avoided liability. Now, however, since passage of The 1991 Civil Rights Act (See the section, following, on Remedies), the employer will be held liable under Title VII. However, under these circumstances, the plaintiff is not entitled to receive monetary damages; her only forms of recovery are an injunction and the payment of her attorney's fees. An employee who refused to submit to sexual advances but who also has a history of poor work performance is an example of a mixed-motive case. Although there are legitimate grounds for dismissing the employee, if she can show that refusal to submit to the advances was contributory to her firing, her employer will be held liable under the 1991 Act.

Hostile Environment Harassment

The guidelines issued by the EEOC, and later adopted in the 1986 Supreme Court case, *Meritor Savings Bank v. Vinson*, recognize that sexually harassing conduct can be so severe or pervasive as to make the workplace unbearable for an employee, thus violating Title VII, even though no tangible job detriment has occurred. In such cases, it is not uncommon for the victim who is harassed to do her job poorly or have excessive absences, resulting in her "active discharge" by her employer. In the alternative, she may be constructively discharged, in which case her work environment becomes so intolerable that she is forced to quit her job. A majority of courts holds an employer liable for constructive discharge when it is foreseeable that the adverse conditions would force a reasonable employee to quit. The employer need not have intended to force the employee to resign.

The *Meritor* case is also important because the decision clarified most of the criteria involving hostile environment cases. Mechelle Vinson was employed as a teller at a Washington, D.C., bank. For four years, based on merit alone, she advanced through positions as head teller and, finally, branch manager. After she was discharged for excessive use of sick leave, she sued the bank and Sidney Taylor, a vice-president, for sexual harassment under Title VII. She testified that during her employment with the bank that she gave in to Taylor's demands for sex over a period of three years for fear of losing her job. In addition, she said Taylor fondled her in front of other employees, followed her into the women's restroom, exposed himself to her, and, more than once, forcibly raped her. Because she feared Taylor, Vinson testified, she never reported his harassment to any of his supervisors or complained using the bank's grievance procedures.

The Supreme Court established in this case that a hostile environment sex discrimination claim could be brought under Title VII. It also established that testimony about the provocative speech and dress of the victim could be introduced in court.

But the Court refused to automatically impose liability on the employer for the creation of a hostile environment by a supervisor or co-worker; employer liability continues to be decided on a case-by-case basis.

*Criteria Used to Determine a Case of Hostile
   Environment Harassment*
The EEOC has stated that since hostile environment harassment takes many forms, some of the factors the Commission will look to in determining whether a Title VII violation has occurred are: 1) whether the conduct was verbal or physical, or both; 2) how frequently it was repeated, 3) whether the conduct was hostile and patently offensive, 4) whether the alleged harasser was a co-worker or a supervisor, 5) whether others joined in perpetrating the harassment, and 6) whether the harassment was directed at more than one individual.

The guidelines state that sexual misconduct is sexual harassment when it has "the purpose or effect of unreasonably interfering with an individual's work performance or creating an intimidating, hostile, or offensive working environment." (*EEOC 1980 Guidelines on Sexual Harassment*, Sec. 1604.11(a)(3)). Minor irritations, such as flirting or the use of vulgar language, even though they are annoying, will probably not establish a hostile environment. Although it is possible to have a single, severe instance of sexual harassment constitute a hostile environment, it is more likely the harassment will have to be pervasive. The more severe the harassment, the less need there is to show a repetitive series of incidents. In particular, intentional touching of a victim's "intimate body areas" is sufficiently offensive to alter the conditions of her working environment. Unlike a *quid pro quo* case in which a single sexual advance, if it is linked to the granting or denial of employment benefits, may qualify as sexual harassment, hostile environment claims generally require a showing of a pattern of offensive conduct.

Sexual harassment need not be physical; it can be verbal or pictorial. The same criteria will be used to evaluate cases of hostile environment harassment as those used to evaluate physical harassment: the nature, frequency, context, and intended target. The Commission will look to the "totality of the circumstances" to determine whether a Title VII violation exists. The U.S. Court of Appeals for the Third Circuit has stated that the plaintiff only needs to show that gender was a substantial factor in her discrimination and that a person of the opposite sex would not have been treated in the same manner. The court held that "the pervasive use of derogatory and insulting terms relating to women generally and addressed to female employees personally may serve as evidence of a hostile environment."[33]

Courts have sometimes analogized sexual harassment that creates a hostile environment to racial harassment that also creates a hostile working environment. As the court in *Henson* stated, "Surely a requirement that a man or woman run a gauntlet of sexual abuse in return for the privilege of being allowed to work and make a living can be as demeaning and disconcerting as the harshest of racial epithets." (p. 902).

Quid Pro Quo Versus Hostile Environment Sexual Harassment

To some extent hostile environment cases overlap with *quid pro quo* cases in that they both involve harassment based on the sex of the victim. In hostile environment cases the discriminatory behavior leads the employee either to quit, and so avoid the offensive contact, or it impairs her ability to do her job so that she is fired for poor performance or for excessive absences. However, the differences between hostile environment cases and *quid pro quo* cases are significant:

1. *Quid pro quo* actions involve behavior by a supervisor; hostile environment actions can be the result of the behavior of a co-worker or a non-employee.
2. *Quid pro quo* claims involve sexual behavior directed at the plaintiff; hostile environment claims may involve non-sexual behavior directed at the plaintiff because of gen-

der. An example of the latter is the director of cafeteria workers who continually demeans only his female workers, telling them they belong in the kitchen and that women are too stupid to hold any other job.

3. *Quid pro quo* claims require resulting economic injury; hostile environment claims require interference with the plaintiff's ability to perform her job due to severe or pervasive sexual harassment.

4. *Quid pro quo* claims usually make the employer liable for harassing actions of a supervisor; in hostile environment claims liability is decided on a case-by-case basis. In hostile environment cases, employers are not always liable for sexual harassment by their supervisors nor is the employer automatically insulated from liability because he has no knowledge of the harassment.[34] The court will look to such factors as whether the employer had a written policy against sexual harassment, whether a grievance mechanism existed, whether the supervisor was acting as an "agent" of his employer, and whether the sexual harassment was pervasive and severe.

As in *quid pro quo* harassment, a display of favoritism may constitute an actionable hostile environment harassment claim. The *EEOC Policy Guide* (January 12, 1990) states, "If favoritism based upon the granting of sexual favors is widespread in a workplace, both male and female colleagues who do not welcome this conduct can establish a hostile work environment in violation of Title VII regardless of whether any objectionable conduct is directed at them and regardless of whether those who were granted favorable treatment willingly bestowed the sexual favors." In this type of situation, the message is conveyed by supervisors that they regard women as sexual objects; as a result, the workplace environment becomes demeaning to women. Both men and women may find the office environment offensive. If the demeaning conduct is sufficiently severe or pervasive to create an abusive and intolerable working environment, both men and women may be able to establish a violation of Title VII. Note, however, that most courts reject the notion that a single office romance that results in favoritism is actionable under Title VII.

When the demeaning conduct is severe, the EEOC likens this situation to an atmosphere in which racial, ethnic or sexual jokes and comments prevail. If the group targeted fails to respond and "plays along" with the speaker of the offensive comments by not protesting the objectionable environment, co-workers of any race or nationality can claim a hostile work environment has been created, since the legal rights of protected class members have been violated.

Evaluating the Severity of the Hostile Environment and the Extent to Which the Plaintiff Has Been Injured

In the case of *Rabidue v. Osceola Refining Company*,[35] Vivenne Rabidue was fired from her job as administrative assistant. She charged the company with sexual harassment as a result of her altercations with Douglas Henry, a co-worker, "an extremely vulgar and crude individual who customarily made obscene comments about women generally, and, on occasion, directed such obscenities to the plaintiff." (p. 615). Other male employees from time to time subjected the plaintiff and other female workers to pictures of nude or scantily-clad women in the work areas where both men and women worked. The court stated that no sexual harassment cause of action under Title VII existed in this case since much of the sexual behavior complained of was not directed at the plaintiff, Vivienne Rabidue. On appeal, the court stated:

> The sexually oriented poster displays had a de minimus effect on the plaintiff's work environment when considered in the context of a society that condones and publicly features and commercially exploits open displays of written and pictorial erotica at newsstands, on primetime television, at the cinema, and in other public places. (p. 622)

More recently, a federal district court in Florida decided a case in which sexually explicit pictures, calendars, centerfolds, and drawings created a hostile work environment for women.[36] Lois Robinson, a welder at Jacksonville Shipyards, was subjected to pornography, sexual "pranks," and sexually explicit comments and graffiti. During her trial experts were permitted to testify on her behalf in regard to the effects of sexual stereotyping and sexual harassment on women. The court found Jacksonville Shipyards liable for the hostile work environment to which Robinson was subjected for not responding to her complaints with prompt remedial measures. It ordered the immediate adoption and implementation of a policy and procedures to prevent and to control sexual harassment.

It might be argued that if a woman enters a job arena dominated by men, she should have to take the situation as she finds it; that rough language and coarse sexual joking and comments are part of the workplace atmosphere; that a woman who can't tolerate explicit sexual language, which will sometimes be directed at her, ought to stay home or take a job in a more ladylike business. Agreeing with the dissent in *Rabidue*, the EEOC contradicted that opinion: ". . .[A] woman does not assume the risk of harassment by voluntarily entering an abusive anti-female environment." (*EEOC Policy Guide* (March 19, 1990)). Quoting Judge Keith in his *Rabidue* dissent: "Title VII's precise purpose is to prevent such behavior and attitudes from poisoning the work environment of classes protected under the Act." (p. 626). Many women decide to enter a profession or job traditionally held by men because their talents and interests lie in that area. For those reasons they may prefer astrobiology to nursing. More likely, however, their reason is economic: welders make more money than waitresses. Economic hardship is also faced by many divorced women, most of whom do not receive alimony. Title VII is a means of assuring each worker, male or female, that he or she will not have to endure an abusive, discriminatory workplace.

Related to the issue of the severity and pervasiveness of the hostile environment is the issue of the extent to which a complainant must be injured in order to prove a violation of Title VII. Lower federal circuit courts were split over the standard that should be applied in assessing injury. Three circuit courts held that the claimant must prove psychological injury resulting from the hostile employment environment.[37] Three other circuit courts did not require psychological injury but only a showing of behavior by the defendant that a reasonable person would find offensive.[38] In a unanimous decision announced in November, 1993, the United States Supreme Court resolved the dis-pute when it decided *Harris v. Forklift Systems, Inc.* In that unanimous decision the Court held that it is unnecessary for employees to prove that sexual harassment severely damaged them psychologically or seriously impaired their work performance in order for them to have an actionable suit against their employer.

Analyzing a Hostile Environment Case

As in Title VII *quid pro quo* cases, an analytical framework is used in hostile environment cases. A major difference, however, involves the shifting burden of proof. In *quid pro quo* cases, after the plaintiff demonstrates that her compliance with sexual behavior was made a condition of her employment or promotion, the burden shifts to the employer to show that the job action taken, for example, a firing, was due to the faulty work performance of the employee. In hostile environment cases, shifting the burden of proof may not be necessary. The unwelcome advances or sexual comments are based on the plaintiff's gender. There is no need for the defense to prove there was no causal link between a firing, for example, and the sexual harassment. The plaintiff shows first that harassing actions took place. (The defendant counters that they did not occur or were insignificant.) Then she must show that the employer took no corrective action, even though he knew about the harassment. (The defendant denies he knew of the harassing actions or says that he did take prompt remedial action.) Thus, there is no shifting of the burden of proof to the defendant.

Lindemann and Kadue, in their book, *Sexual Harassment in Employment Law*,[39] state that in a hostile environment case, the plaintiff must first show:

1) *Membership in a protected group.* Actions may be brought either by men or by women since the law was intended to protect both sexes.
2) *Unwelcome conduct of a sexual [sex-based] nature.* The conduct can be teasing or hazing based on gender. It may also be crude, sexual language or behavior, posters, pictures, cartoons, or drawings. The significant criterion is that the action is unwelcome to the plaintiff and that it occurred because of her gender.
3) *The unwelcome conduct affected a term and condition of employment.* The behavior complained of must be either severe or pervasive enough to create a truly abusive work environment. Occasional vulgar language or dirty jokes are insufficient to maintain a cause of action. The court will look to the totality of the circumstances in making a determination of whether the harassment was sufficiently severe or pervasive. That will include who was harassing (for example, a supervisor may have greater capacity to create a hostile environment) and whether other workers joined in the harassment.
4) *The conduct was on the basis of sex.* Here, the complainant must show that the harassment would not have occurred except for her sex. The complaint may be based on unwanted sexual advances, disparaging comments reflecting on the plaintiff's gender, or on a "sexually-charged" workplace (the posting of pornographic pictures and graffiti, for example).
5) *Employer responsibility.* Employers are neither automatically liable nor automatically protected from liability in hostile environment cases.

Employer Liability for the Acts of Employees in Hostile Environment Cases

Some confusion remains in hostile environment cases regarding when an employer will be liable for the sexually harassing behavior of an employee. If a school hires an eighteen-year-old woman to drive a school bus and the administrator in charge of the buses makes suggestive comments to her, phones her at home, and tries to fondle her in the bus parking lot, what is the principal's or the school district's liability for the actions of the administrator? The issue is less clear in this case than in *quid pro quo* cases where the employer will assume direct liability for the actions of its supervisors. The Court in *Meritor* declined to issue a definitive rule on employer liability in hostile environment cases. But it did add that Congress, by defining "employer" to include any "agent" of an employer, evinced "an intent to place some limits on the acts of employees for which employers under Title VII are to be held responsible." (p. 72). The Court then held that employers are not always automatically liable for sexual harassment by their supervisors. But at the same time, the Court added, the absence of notice to an employer does not necessarily insulate that employer from liability.

How might a complainant demonstrate that an employer had actual or constructive notice in a hostile-environment case? Recent federal court decisions in both the district courts and in the courts of appeal[40] have enumerated the types of issues courts will be focusing on when they evaluate the school district's liability for the sexually harassing behavior of its employees:

> 1. *Did the employer have a strenuous anti-discrimination policy and an accessible grievance procedure to insure that it would be informed of offensive behavior?* The EEOC policy forbids an employer from deliberately turning its back on the problem of sexual harassment by failing to establish a policy against it and a grievance mechanism to redress it.

2. *How pervasive and how severe was the harassment?* If everyone in the school knew of the harassment, it will be difficult for the employer to deny it did not know, regardless whether the employee reported the incident to a supervisor. Testimony by co-workers who knew of the harassment will be persuasive in a courtroom.

3. *Once it was put on notice or his suspicions were aroused, did the employer investigate the alleged harassment?* Information may come from other employees, parents, students, or even the police. School districts may incur liability for failure to take immediate and effective action once harassment is known or suspected.

4. *When it did investigate the alleged behavior, did the employer keep accurate records of his investigation and any subsequent action taken?* Investigative work is without value if there are no permanent records of the procedure, the findings, and any disciplinary action taken.

5. *Was it foreseeable that this employee would sexually harass another school employee?* Increasingly, courts are demanding that employers not only remediate the situation once sexual harassment has occurred, but that they also take preventive measures to see that it does not happen in the first place. An employer who knows of previous misconduct by an employee has a duty to insure that the misconduct does not recur. In the school context, it is in the school district's best interest to thoroughly investigate the background of all potential employees. If a present employee has been disciplined for sexually discriminatory behavior, the school must follow up on that employee to see the behavior is not repeated.

The Supreme Court emphasized in *Meritor* (p. 72) that "the mere existence of a grievance procedure and a policy against discrimination, coupled with [the victim's] failure to invoke the procedure" are "plainly relevant" but "not necessarily dispositive."

How would the court decide the case of the harassed female bus driver? A decision could well hinge on whether an adequate grievance procedure existed in the school district, what action the school district took following the harassment, how quickly it attempted to remedy the grievance, and whether the school district had prior knowledge of the employee's propensity for sexual harassment.

A Hostile Environment in the School Setting

The likelihood of school principals and other school personnel papering their walls with pornography and subjecting teachers and other school personnel to pinups and calendars with nearly-nude models seems remote. Hostile environment cases may have relevance to the schools in related contexts, however. Title IX cases tend to track those of Title VII. (Title IX is discussed in a subsequent section.) Causes of action applicable in the workplace may also be applicable in the school setting in which students, rather than employees, are involved. For example, offensive sexual graffiti about a student, written on schoolroom walls or restroom walls, may present a case of hostile environment. In particular, if the school has notice of the graffiti and fails to remove it, the school district increases its chances of being found liable under a hostile environment cause of action.

Hostile environment liability may arise even for the conduct of non-employees, such as independent contractors, unless the employer exercises reasonable control to prevent the harassment or to remediate it. This type of third person harassment is more common in jobs involving clients or customers. Typically, the employee is harassed by the client; when the employee refuses to acquiesce to the sexual advances of the client, the client may complain to the employer that its employee is "uncooperative." Sometimes the employee is then fired. A case now pending in U.S. District Court in New York involves an account supervisor at an advertising agency who alleges she was sexually harassed by a client and was later fired by her employer upon the demand of the client. In a $2.2 million dollar suit, the advertising agency, the client, and the client's employer are being sued for sexual harassment and defamation.

The significant criterion in assessing cases of harassment by a non-employee is whether the school district knew or should have known of the sexual harassment and whether, once they were informed, they took corrective action. If the school is apprised that sexual harassment is occurring, responsive action should not include moving the employee to another location or to a less desirable job. Courts will carefully scrutinize the motives of the employer in such a case. The appropriate response is to inform the non-employee, a delivery person, for example, that his offensive behavior must cease; if that action is ineffective, the school district should inform the company for whom he works and demand that the offensive behavior stop. In extreme cases, the school district should find another company to deal with.

Third person suits in a school district may be less likely than in a large corporation, but the potential for injury exists. In one case, a school district hired a construction company to perform extensive repairs on a school building during the summer months when no students or teachers were present in the building. The construction company was from out of state and its workers were from various parts of the country. Throughout the summer, workers were sometimes present in the teachers' lounges as well as in the restrooms of male and female faculty members. By the end of the summer, construction was complete, and students and teachers returned to their renovated building. However, the workers left the restroom walls etched with particularly graphic obscenities. Eighty percent of the faculty were women, and some of them complained to the principal about being subjected to these obscenities several times a day. Despite numerous complaints, the obscenities remained until the restrooms were painted over a year later.

The attitude of the courts in hostile environment cases was summarized by the United States Court of Appeals for the

Ninth Circuit in 1989.[41] The court declared that the prevailing trend is to hold employers liable for failure to take prompt corrective action to remedy a hostile or offensive work environment of which "management-level" employees knew, or in the exercise of reasonable care should have known. As employers, schools have the same obligation as corporations to insure that the work environment is not only safe but non-discriminatory as well.

Can the policy that forbids employers from maintaining a hostile environment be extended a step further to protect students who are subjected to obscene graffiti, language, and behavior even though this form of sexual harassment is not directed at a particular individual? If the sexually harassing environment is severe and pervasive and if a school fails to respond to students' complaints, the school district could find itself liable, under a related statute, for its inaction. That statute (Title IX) is discussed in a later section of this book.

Federal Law: Remedies Under the Civil Rights Act of 1964 and Under the Civil Rights Act of 1991

Relief Available Under the Civil Rights Act of 1964

Injunctive Relief

Most victims of sexual harassment want primarily one thing: they want the harassment to stop. If victims are unable to stop it themselves and their employers are unwilling to stop it, victims may resort to litigation. A remedial device available to the court is the injunction, an order directing a person to perform an action or to refrain from performing it. The types of actions that may be enjoined are sexually harassing conduct, refusal by an employer to investigate complaints, or refusal to establish a grievance procedure. The court may also order a person or a corporation not to retaliate against an employee who complains. It should be noted that various federal and state laws specifically prohibit retaliation.

Generally, injunctions are issued only if the employee is still working for her employer. However, a few exceptions exist. For example, an injunction to prevent retaliation against a former employee who has filed a complaint with the EEOC may be issued if the employee has a legal action pending against the employer. The injunction is authorized by section 706(g) of Title VII if the court finds "intentional" unlawful employment practices. The term "intentional" has generally been interpreted by the courts to mean that the employment practices are non-accidental. Most courts focus on the consequences of an employer's actions rather than on his motive. Previously, injunctive relief was the only form of relief available unless a victim could prove tangible economic loss. Some victims, because they were without recourse, endured sexual harassment for years.

Employees are also entitled to future and continued injunctive relief unless the employer has demonstrated satisfactorily to the court that the harassment has ended. More is expected of an employer, however, than a glib statement that he "won't do it anymore." The court will want tangible reassurance.

Section 706(g) also authorizes courts to "order such affirmative action as may be appropriate." A comprehensive example of such relief was ordered by the court in *Robinson v. Jacksonville Shipyards*. A partial list of rehabilitative measures ordered by the court in that case included: to post a list of offenses and behaviors that constitute sexual harassment, to adopt a list of penalties for misconduct (ranging from counseling to dismissal), to provide a mechanism for reporting incidents of sexual harassment, to appoint and to train investigative officers, and to provide sanctions for officials who retaliated against complainants. Courts may also provide for monitoring and other follow-up procedures of the offending employer.

In addition to injunctive relief, a court may order reinstatement, with no loss of seniority, to a victim of sexual harassment. It can also order that a victim be promoted, transferred, or given a job title.

Note that injunctive relief may be available before a complainant's case is tried in court. Under the laws of some states, the complainant may get an immediate protective order.

Money Damages

Section 706(g), in addition to providing injunctive relief, also provides "back pay" and "other equitable relief as the court deems appropriate." (The 1991 Act provides additional forms of monetary relief--see the following section.) Courts traditionally rely on case law from other Title VII, non-sexual harassment suits, such as racial discrimination cases, to determine the appropriate relief in sexual harassment cases. A problem arises in hostile environment cases where the complainant has not gained or lost a benefit due to the sexual advances of an employer since she was not actually or constructively discharged. In these cases the plaintiff will not have suffered a tangible economic loss and thus will not be able to claim back pay.

Back pay also includes cost-of-living increases, raises, annual leave and sick pay, pension and retirement benefits, and insurance. A teacher, for example, who is paid over the summer and who accumulates sick leave and retirement benefits would still be owed those benefits should it be decided her case has merit. Interest is usually awarded, too, both pre- and post-judgment, and will be calculated according to the discretion of the court.

The Act places a limit on how far into the past back pay accrues. The limit is no more than two years before the EEOC charge was filed. For example, if a school secretary was fired for refusing to give in to her employer's demands for sexual relations, the date of her firing would be the determinative day at which she could begin to calculate back pay. If a male teacher was denied a promotion because he resisted his male principal's advances, the day the promised promotion would have gone into effect would be the day his back pay began to accrue. In a hostile environment case, if peer harassment by a fellow teacher led to a teacher's constructive discharge, (that is, the harasser made her work environment intolerable, forcing her to quit), the day of her constructive discharge would be the determinative day for beginning back-pay. In all the above examples, however, the two-year statute of limitations on back-pay is applicable.

The back-pay period ends with the resolution of the case, for example, when the judgment of the court is rendered. If a school district reinstates an employee, or grants her the promotion she has been denied, or transfers her to another school, the back-pay period will end on that day.

Note than an employee is expected to look for another job with "reasonable diligence" during the period she is out of work. The amount earned from a new job will be deducted from the amount she is due from the school district. Should she have the good fortune to earn more than the amount she would have earned from the school, back-pay will be denied. If the employer has caused the victim to incur psychological damage as a result of the harassment, some courts may be more lenient on a victim for failing to find a new job.

A plaintiff who prevails in a Title VII case may also recover reasonable attorneys fees. These fees can be considerable. Prior to the recent increase in monetary damages now available to a plaintiff, most attorneys worked only on a straight hourly-fee basis. In a case accepted on a contingency basis, the lawyer contracts with the client to take a percentage of the award made by the court, usually one-third. Should the case go to trial, rather than settling, the attorney may claim as much as fifty percent of the client's award. In addition, the prevailing party in employment discrimination cases may usually receive court costs. Costs include such fees as those for the court reporter, for witnesses, or for copying necessary papers.

Courts also have the discretion to award sums of money unconnected to back-pay. A few courts have awarded "front-pay." That is an amount payable where an employee merits reinstatement, but no suitable position is available or where it would be undesirable for a former employee to work for the same employer again. The amount of front-pay is the difference between the salary of a new job with lower pay and the salary at the employee's former position. The pay continues until salary at the new job is on a par with the salary of the previous job. Other courts have awarded actual damages, a lump-sum payment to the employee in recognition of medical costs, including psychological counseling. A federal court in Florida recently decided a case in which a female employee suffered *quid pro quo* harassment, hostile environment harassment, and constructive discharge.[42] In addition, the woman had several state law claims. The court awarded her front-pay, $250,000 in compensatory damages, and $1,000,000 punitive damages. (See the following section for a discussion of compensatory and punitive damages available under Title VII.)

Relief Available Under the Civil Rights Act of 1991

In addition to injunctive relief and the monetary damages listed in the preceding sections, the amended Civil Rights Act of 1991 provides that a party who proves "intentional discrimination" may also recover compensatory and punitive damages. Compensatory damages, unavailable prior to 1991, reimburse the plaintiff for her actual losses (for example, medical bills) incurred by a worker as a result of sexual harassment. Compensatory damages are awarded for the purpose of compensating the damaged party for pain and suffering, future money losses and other non-monetary losses. Punitive damages are intended to punish the offender and to make an example of him. In order to receive punitive damages, the plaintiff must prove that the employer discriminated "with malice or with reckless indifference" to the rights of the offended party.

Under the 1991 Civil Rights Act, although these additional monetary damages are now available, there is a ceiling on the amount that a victim may recover, depending on the total number of employees in the company or institution. The figures below represent the total number of employees in a school district, not the number employed in a single school. The number includes not only teachers and administrators but also such employees as clerical workers, cafeteria workers, clean-up personnel, and bus drivers.

Number of Employees	Total Damages Available
15-100	$50,000
101-200	$100,000
201-500	$200,000
more than 500	$300,000

Jurors would not be informed of the cap on damages. In theory, they could award a greater amount of damages than that specified in the Act. However, that amount would then be reduced by the judge to keep within the limits of the statute. Legislation now pending in Congress would remove these caps.

Several other features of the Civil Rights Act of 1991 bear mentioning. Any party (the alleged harasser or a claimant) can now demand a jury trial when compensatory or punitive damages are requested. Many plaintiffs and their attorneys believe the likelihood of winning a case and of receiving larger damage awards is greater when the case is tried to a jury rather than heard by a judge alone. The Act also provides that an award of reasonable attorney's fees may include an award of expert fees. An expert might be called in a sexual harassment case to testify to the psychological effect of harassment on a victim.

Finally, in cases of "mixed motives," where a claimant has proved sexual harassment and the employer has shown he would have taken the same negative job action, even without a discriminatory motive, a violation of Title VII has been demonstrated. Prior to the 1991 Act, the claimant would have lost her case.

Filing a Claim with the EEOC
To use the Civil Rights Act, one must file a claim with the EEOC and obtain a right-to-sue letter from it before proceeding with a complaint. In most states a complainant can file with

the state or local Fair Employment Practices agency (FEP) and simultaneously have her grievance filed with the EEOC. A computer link is maintained between the federal and state agency. These "dual-filing" agreements work the opposite way as well. A case filed with the EEOC is simultaneously filed with the FEP. Although only one investigation takes place, the dual-filing is beneficial to the claimant, who is then able to take advantage of both the Civil Rights Act and the state FEP law. Claimants may also pursue the grievance procedure at their companies or through their labor unions at the same time they are filing a federal or a state claim.

Unless the EEOC or FEP advises otherwise, the time period for filing a claim is within 180 days of the incident of sexual harassment. In some cases, by state statute, a claimant may be granted up to 240 days or 300 days to file a charge with the EEOC. It is best to check with the state office of the EEOC for deadlines, since a claim may be lost if it is not filed within the prescribed period of time. The deadline is not extended if a claimant is following a company's grievance procedure. Under rare, extenuating circumstances, such as the complainant's severe illness, the EEOC may extend the time period for filing a claim. The claim must be in writing, and it is usually best to go to the FEP agency or EEOC office in person. After a charge is filed, the senior manager of the EEOC office will review it to determine how the charge will be processed. Within ten days, the EEOC will notify the employer and anyone else charged that a discrimination complaint has been filed. The employer is then asked to confer with the EEOC for a fact-finding investigation. Thereafter, an attempt will be made to settle the complaint between the employer and the employee.

If a lengthier investigation is called for and the EEOC reaches a "no-cause" decision, the complainant has three courses of action available: 1) she may appeal the decision, 2) she may treat the decision as a right-to-sue letter and litigate the case, or 3) she may accept the EEOC decision and do nothing. Regardless of the outcome of the EEOC investigation, a claimant may take her case to court. However, a finding of no-cause by the EEOC usually dissuades claimants from litigation. In a few cases, if it finds cause, the EEOC may litigate the case itself. In states where the EEOC has exclusive jurisdiction, it has 180 days to complete its investigation. If it is not completed within that time, a complainant may demand a right-to-sue letter. In those states with state deferral agencies, where a complaint is filed with the state agency, such as the civil rights office, and simultaneously with the EEOC, a claimant may request a right-to-sue letter from the state agency after 60 days have elapsed from the date of filing. From the date the right-to-sue letter is received, the complainant has 90 days to file a lawsuit. A plaintiff may be barred from suing under Title VII unless she files suit within that time period. The EEOC stops its investigation when the letter is issued. It is crucial for a complainant to pay close attention to all dates so that her case is not barred by failure to bring suit within the specified statute of limitations.

Non-Retaliation Requirements

An important provision of the Civil Rights Act of 1964 is its warning against retaliation toward an employee who has reported an instance of discrimination or who has cooperated in an investigation. The EEOC should be notified if any attempt at retaliation is made. Section 704(a) of the Civil Rights Act states:

> It shall be unlawful employment practice for an employer to discriminate against any of his employees or applicants for employment, for an employment agency to discriminate against any individual, or for a labor organization to discriminate against any member thereof or applicant for membership, because he has opposed a practice made an unlawful employment practice by this title or because he has made a charge, testified, assisted, or participated in any manner in an investigation, proceeding, or hearing under this title.

From Whose Point of View?

One area of the law courts have wrestled with in sexual harassment cases is the point of view from which sexual harassment should be perceived. The issue may be phrased: If sexual harassment happens primarily to women, and if men and women perceive the same sexual conduct differently, then shouldn't cases of sexual harassment be decided from a woman's point of view? Traditionally, the perspective used by juries in a civil suit has been that of the hypothetical "reasonable person," which is to say, the reasonable man.

There are numerous reasons for the adoption of the reasonable man standard. First, it is an attempt to make the matters presented to the jury seem logical. Its use emphasizes to the jury that they are to decide a case based on what the average person would have done in a similar situation. Second, the use of the reasonable man is an attempt to draw the jury's attention away from the unique perspective of the defendant and to discourage them from individualizing their decision. It is an attempt to get the jury to focus their deliberations not on, Why did *this* man do this act?, but what would a *reasonable* man have done in the same circumstances? With a few exceptions, notably for those defendants with physical impairments and for children, the reasonable man has been the standard in American law for almost 150 years. Finally, the most obvious reason for the adoption of the reasonable man standard is that until the latter half of the twentieth century not all states had women on their juries; therefore, there was no justification for regarding a defendant from any perspective other than that of a reasonable man's.

Cases of rape and of sexual harassment present troublesome issues when the victim is considered from the perspective of the reasonable man. Since rape and sexual harassment occur primarily to women, would a reasonable man and a reasonable woman behave in the same manner when confronted with these offenses? If they would respond differently, should the standard used by jurors in evaluating defendant culpability still be that of a reasonable man? Are there cultural and sociological differences that prompt different responses from men and women confronted with the same circumstances? The courts have confronted these issues and the development of a reasonable woman standard is emerging in their published opinions.

In 1986, in *Rabidue v. Osceola Refining Company*, a hostile environment case, Judge Keith of the Sixth Circuit wrote a dissent that is more memorable today than the opinion of the court. In that dissent he wrote,

> In my view, the reasonable person perspective fails to account for the wide divergence between most women's views of appropriate sexual conduct and those of men. . .unless the outlook of the reasonable woman is adopted, the defendants as well as the courts are permitted to sustain ingrained notions of reasonable behavior fashioned by the offenders, in this case, men.
>
> . . .[T]he relevant inquiry at hand is what the reasonable woman would find offensive, not society, which at one point also condoned slavery. I conclude that sexual posters and anti-female language can seriously affect the psychological well being of the reasonable woman and interfere with her ability to perform her job. (p.626-627)

More recently, the ninth circuit, in *Ellison v. Brady*,[43] adopted the reasonable woman standard in a hostile environment case. Kerry Ellison worked as a revenue agent for the Internal Revenue Service in San Mateo, California. A co-worker, Sterling Gray, began to pester Ellison, hanging around her desk and inviting her to lunch. Even though she refused his advances, he continued to send her bizarre notes and letters, implying they had a romantic relationship. Ellison had kept her supervisor apprised of Gray's behavior, telling her that Gray's actions were frightening her. The supervisor warned Gray to stay away from Ellison. Shortly after Gray had transferred to San Francisco, the IRS permitted him to return to work in the office where Ellison continued to work. Frantic by this time, Ellison filed a formal complaint and Gray once more wrote her a "love letter." Although the Treasury Department rejected Ellison's complaint, the Court of Appeals held that Ellison had stated a cause of action for a hostile environment sexual harassment case.

Judge Beezer's decision in that case analyzed harassment from the victim's perspective. He noted that an understanding from the victim's view required an analysis of the different perspectives of men and women. Even though the harasser might unintentionally create a hostile working environment, he would still be held liable. "Well-intentioned compliments by co-workers or supervisors can form the basis of a sexual harassment cause of action if a reasonable victim of the same sex as the plaintiff would consider the comments sufficiently severe or pervasive to alter a condition of employment and create an abusive working environment." (p. 880)

Additionally, the *EEOC Compliance Manual* suggests that the offensive conduct should be judged from the viewpoint of the female employee. At the same time, the Manual states, it is in a woman's best interest to speak up when she is offended and not to "play along" with the harasser.

Currently, the application of the reasonable woman criterion is more widespread than it was a decade ago. However, until the reasonable woman standard is consistent throughout the country, the perspective applied in a hostile environment case will depend on the part of the country in which the case is being tried.

Federal Law: Education Amendment of 1972, Title IX--Federal Aid to Schools

Title IX of the Education Amendments of 1972 provides that:

> No person in the United States shall, on the basis of sex, be excluded from participation in, be denied the benefits of, or be subjected to discrimination under any education program or activity receiving Federal financial assistance.
>
> (20 U.S.C. Sec. 1681(a))

Three criteria must be met before an institution can be held in violation of Title IX. The institution's program or activity

1) Must be educational. Title IX coverage extends to *any* educational program receiving federal financial assistance, whether or not a school or school district sponsors the program. Such informal programs as 4-H Clubs and on-the-job training programs are included.
2) Must receive federal funds. Most private as well as public schools receive federal funds. Regardless of whether the objectionable acts occurred in a program that was federally funded, if *any* program in the school receives federal assistance, then the school may be held liable under Title IX.
3) Must engage in discrimination on the basis of sex. As in Title VII, the statute does not define sex discrimination. Regulations and interpretations of Title IX by the courts have included discrimination on the basis of parental or marital status, discrimination in athletics, discrimination in course offerings, discrimination in counseling students, discrimination in admissions policies, discrimination in employment, and sexual harassment.

The U.S. Department of Education, in an August 1981 policy memorandum issued to all Regional Civil Rights Directors, reaffirmed its jurisdiction over sexual harassment complaints under Title IX and defined sexual harassment in the following manner:

> Sexual harassment consists of verbal or physical conduct of a sexual nature, imposed on the basis of sex, by an employee or agent of a recipient that denies, limits, provides different, or conditions the provision of aid, benefits, services or treatment protected under Title IX.

Discrimination under Title IX on the basis of gender applies to all students and employees, including full- and part-time workers. Thus, Title IX covers discrimination in employment decisions and educational opportunities. Since Title VII is better known and the law under that statute is more fully developed, an employee is more likely to seek protection under Title VII. Students, who are not covered by Title VII, may bring suit under Title IX. The courts have interpreted that statute by adopting many of the principles from Title VII and the caselaw that has evolved from that statute. Courts have ruled that Title IX prohibits both *quid pro quo* sexual harassment and hostile environment harassment.

There are two aspects of sex discrimination addressed by Title IX. 1) It obligates the school to maintain a non-discriminatory learning environment and helps to enforce the opportunity for an equal education for all students regardless of gender. 2) It impacts on each individual student's educational program and progress.

Unlike Title VII, which is enforced through the EEOC, Title IX is enforced through the federal Office for Civil Rights (OCR). That Office enforces four federal statutes that prohibit discrimination in programs and activities that receive federal financial assistance from the U.S. Department of Education: Title VI, which prohibits discrimination on the basis of race, color, and national origin; Title IX, which prohibits discrimination on the basis of sex; Section 504 of the Rehabilitation Act of 1973, which prohibits discrimination on the basis of handicap; and the Age Discrimination Act of 1975, which prohibits discrimination on the basis of age. As in Title VII cases, those institutions against whom a complaint has been filed with OCR may not retaliate against any person who has made a complaint or participated in any manner in an investigation under the four statutes listed above. Title IX may also be enforced through civil litigation. In any case, the complaining party must demonstrate that the institution is a federally-funded educational institution that engaged in discrimination on the basis of sex.

Under Title IX, suit is brought against the educational institution rather than against the individual who allegedly discriminated against the complaining party. Of course, a person may bring suit against the actual perpetrator on the basis of other state or federal law. Title IX regulations require the school to apprise employees, students, and their parents that the school and/or school district do not discriminate on the basis of sex in its educational programs or activities. The school district must publish a policy on sex discrimination and inform each employee and student of its existence and substance. It must also provide adequate grievance procedures to receive, investigate, and resolve complaints. School districts can be found liable under Title IX if they failed to take any of the above steps.

Filing a Complaint Under Title IX

Students or school personnel with a complaint of discrimination on the basis of sex, or sexual harassment specifically, should be encouraged to resolve the problem informally by speaking to their grievance counselor or Title IX coordinator. Most complaints go no further than this stage, and an equitable solution satisfactory to all parties is generally reached. Although the position of the Title IX Coordinator is mandated by the statute, in most districts the job is handled by an employee who also serves in another capacity, such as the personnel director. However, complainants are not required to follow their district's grievance procedure prior to filing a complaint with OCR. If the complainant follows the district's procedures and remains unsatisfied, she must file a complaint with OCR within 60 days after completing the last act of the district's grievance process. The OCR investigation is then limited to those allegations raised pursuant to the district's grievance procedure.

In those states that have provisions in their statutes similar to the anti-discrimination prohibitions found in Title IX, the state Human Rights Commission or state Civil Rights Commission will investigate the complaints that are based on the state statute. As in Title VII cases, the Commission will investigate the complaint, but unlike the procedure followed in Title VII cases, the Commission does not issue a right-to-sue letter. The complainant may file suit in the absence of such a letter. The Commission will, however, try to resolve the complaint and can attempt conciliation between the complainant and the district. Outcomes of conciliation may range from the school district's implementation of a policy and procedure for filing grievances to the payment of a monetary settlement to the victim. It is important for a complainant to check with her state civil rights commission to determine whether a complaint may be filed with them or whether she needs to go directly to the federal Office for Civil Rights. If her state civil rights agency accepts a complaint based on state law, a victim may also file her federal complaint simultaneously with the Regional Office for Civil Rights.

A third means of filing a complaint under Title IX is for the victim of discrimination to send a report to the Regional Office for Civil Rights. (See Appendix for locations of Regional Offices.) It must be filed no later than 180 days from the date of the alleged discrimination, unless the time is extended by OCR for "good cause." The report must be in writing, either in letter form or on the special form provided by OCR. Information required includes:

1) Name, address, and daytime phone number (if possible);
2) A general description of the person(s) or class of persons injured by the alleged discriminatory act(s).Names of the injured person are not required. Complaints may be filed by anyone on behalf of another;
3) The name and location of the school or district that committed the alleged discriminatory act(s); and
4) A description of the act(s) in detail so that OCR can understand what happened, when it happened, and the basis for alleging discrimination based on sex.

OCR attempts to maintain the confidentiality of the complainant. It does not reveal the name of the victim unless it is necessary to complete an inquiry or to comply with the law.

OCR has 90 days to investigate a complaint, followed by another 90 days for negotiation of a voluntary compliance agreement. In practice, investigations often take longer. The investigation consists of the collection and analysis of information to determine whether there is a violation of the laws OCR enforces. Most often it will attempt to resolve matters informally. OCR then prepares a report, which includes recommendations for corrective action, if needed. If OCR finds violations, it not only specifies corrective action but will also monitor the school to assure compliance with the agreed-upon remediation. If OCR finds that discrimination has occurred and no agreement can be reached, it may begin proceedings to terminate the federal funds allocated to that school. OCR may also refer the case to the Department of Justice for possible initiation of legal action against the district.

Besides receiving complaints from individuals, OCR also conducts compliance reviews to insure enforcement of civil rights laws that come under the auspices of OCR. The procedures applicable to Title VII of the Civil Rights Act of 1964 also apply to Title IX. (See 34 CFR 100.6-100.11 and 34 CFR Part 101.) Each school district must provide reports to its state department of education containing information about participation in programs receiving federal assistance, broken down by race, ethnicity, and sex. Those reports are then furnished to OCR, which determines whether schools are complying with the statute. As in cases of non-compliance reported by individuals, if a school district is not in compliance, it may be penalized by having its federal funds suspended or terminated or by other means "authorized by law." OCR may refer the case to the Department of Justice to bring proceedings under federal, state, or local law. Besides relying on information provided by individual schools, OCR also receives information from interest groups, the media and the general public. The Office will provide technical assistance to aid school districts in their voluntary compliance with civil rights laws. Their publications on various civil rights topics are available to schools and to the public.

Remedies for injured employees under Title IX, similar to those available under Title VII, may include injunctive relief, employment or reinstatement, back pay and benefits, interest, attorneys' fees, assurances of future compliance, and monetary damages. For students, remedies may include injunctive relief, reassignment and training of an offending instructor in matters relating to discrimination based on sex, attorneys' fees, and monetary damages. Suit by the government could result in injunctive relief, monetary damages, and attorneys' fees. Special notice should be taken that a Title IX complaint must be filed within 180 days of the date of the alleged discrimination.

A victim may bypass the above procedures and file a suit in federal court. To recover monetary damages in a private action, the victim must prove that the school intentionally discriminated against her on the basis of sex and that she suffered actual damage as a result. The victim need not prove that school officials conspired to discriminate in order to establish intent; most courts require only proof that the discrimination was not accidental and that school officials refused to take action when they knew of the discrimination.

School District Liability and
Considerations in the School Setting

Under Title IX, institutions must adopt and publish procedures for prompt and effective resolution of complaints. Since there are as yet no Title IX OCR guidelines comparable to Title VII EEOC guidelines, educational institutions are expected to develop their own policies and procedures. The care with which these Title IX mandates are monitored varies from state to state.

Once a school district adopts and publishes its complaint procedures, it is obligated to see that they are enforced. The procedures are required to be accessible to students and to employees. The school district must diligently investigate allegations of discrimination, and it must equitably resolve conflicts and punish offenders. The district should have a follow-up procedure in place to insure that incidents of sexual harassment do not recur.

School districts may be held liable under Title IX as an employer. Under this theory, the district is responsible for the acts of its administrators, supervisors, or "agents." This is true regardless whether the school was aware of the harassment and even if it had a policy prohibiting sexual harassment. In determining school district liability, teachers are considered "supervisory," and, therefore, the school district, under Title IX, may be liable for teachers' sexually harassing actions toward students. Schools may also be held liable for acts of co-workers, where the school district knew or should have know of the harassing behavior but failed to take effective corrective action. This same criteria may be applied to non-employees, such as repair workers, suppliers, and delivery people. Since Title IX protects students as well as employees, the school could also be held liable for offensive behavior directed toward students. An important criterion in assessing potential liability is the remedial action taken by the school or district once it became aware of the behavior.

Title IX applies to all federally-funded schools--colleges as well as high schools, middle schools, and elementary schools. Although thousands of discrimination suits have been brought against colleges, relatively few have been brought by students against elementary through secondary schools. Contributing factors are that younger students are generally less well informed about their rights under the law, and they may fear their complaints will not be taken seriously. Increasingly, however, more suits are being brought under Title IX for sexual harassment by elementary and high school students.

In 1977, an undergraduate woman at Yale University charged that she received a lower grade on a paper and in a course because she refused her male professor's advances.[44] Four other students and a male professor joined her suit and stated that because Yale was tolerating sexual pressures on students, an atmosphere resulted in which teaching and learning were inhibited. The suit asked for an adequate grievance procedure at Yale. Ultimately, all complaints were dismissed; however, Yale complied with student demands for a grievance procedure. The most important result of the case is that the court decision stated that sexual harassment could constitute sex discrimination prohibited under Title IX.

Although fewer cases of sexual harassment are reported by students in middle school and high school, this does not mean there is less harassment. On the contrary, there are probably many more occurrences of harassment in schools than in the workplace. A difference between harassment in the workplace and harassment in the schools is that the offensive behavior in schools is more likely to occur between peers rather than between teachers and students or between other school personnel and students. As a result, complaints are less likely to be taken seriously. Title VII is also a more widely-known statute than Title IX and the caselaw is more fully developed; therefore, more suits are filed under Title VII. Since Title VII is inapplicable to students, their only avenue to redress complaints under federal law may be Title IX. Misconceptions about Title IX contribute to the infrequency of its use. Many people associate Title IX only with high school athletics and the statute's requirement mandating that young women be given the opportunity to participate equally with young men in sports programs. The school setting poses unique problems for students. These problems may account for the fact that sexual harassment is reported less in the schools than in the workplace.

The victims of harassment in schools are all young, generally between the ages of 11 and 18. They are socially less experienced than women in the workplace. Aside from merely feeling "uncomfortable" with the harasser's behavior, they may not be able to articulate precisely what the harasser is doing. If the school does not educate students about sexual harassment and does not provide and encourage an avenue of complaint, they may feel they have no recourse other than to try to cope with the harassment on their own. They are often too embarrassed to tell a parent or other adult who could help them understand that they are being sexually harassed, or they may feel that they are somehow responsible for the harasser's actions.

Schools have traditionally tolerated "rambunctious" behavior from students. Touching and teasing of girls by boys and vice versa may be an everyday occurrence at school. The boys chase the girls and the girls chase the boys. When students squeal or complain to their teachers, their complaints are normally dismissed. Middle school and junior high school teachers, in particular, often joke and roll their eyes in mock dismay about an excess of "hormones" in their students. Pinching and poking and name-calling is often viewed as part of a developmental stage that boys and girls will outgrow. But the fact that a great deal of the harassing behavior persists after high school and continues into the workplace demonstrates that much of it is never outgrown.

Another problem sexually harassed students face is that they are in school for a short period of time. In addition to the expense and emotional turmoil of a lawsuit, they may not be willing to initiate a case that can drag on for years. Groups of students involved in litigation find it difficult to maintain cohesiveness over a period of years. As a result, schools may be less likely to take their complaints seriously.

From the school district's perspective, it may fear that wide dissemination of a policy against sexual harassment may jeopardize desirable teacher-student relationships and closeness, ultimately destroying them. Many middle school and high school teachers fill a role somewhere between a close friend and the ideal parent. This relationship is often seen as central to the learning process. Students and teachers are more likely to have an emotional component in their relationship, whereas employees and employers are more apt to have a professional and job-oriented relationship. Given a choice between destroying good relationships and "stirring up trouble" when there may not be any sexual harassment in their school, many school officials refuse to implement a sexual harassment policy.

Damages Under Title IX

Title IX does not specifically provide for an award of monetary damages for a victim of sex discrimination. The means to achieving these damages followed a tortuous path, ultimately leading to a United States Supreme Court decision in February 1992, in which the court concluded that damages could be awarded under Title IX to those who had been discriminated against on the basis of sex, including those who had been sexually harassed.

In a case arising in the Seventh Circuit,[45] the U.S. Supreme Court held that Title IX contains an implied right of action for an individual injured by a violation of that statute. Before this case, an institution could be deprived of federal funds if it generally discriminated on the basis of sex, but individuals had no means of redressing their injuries. The explanation for permitting individuals to bring suit is that Congress would not have created a statute unless it also intended that there be some relief available to vindicate the rights granted individuals by the statute. Originally, Title IX provided injunctive relief to a victim, and it still does. Injunctive relief, however, does not compensate a victim, nor does it deter the defendant and others similarly situated from committing future discriminatory acts. For compensation and deterrence, monetary damages are most effective. A school district that violates the Act and is forced to pay monetary damages will have to divert funds to the plaintiff that might ordinarily go to improved school programs, teachers' salaries, and plant maintenance. Thus, paying damages not only creates an economic hardship for the school district, it also angers taxpayers who support the schools.

Prior to the U.S. Supreme Court case of 1992, lower federal courts were divided regarding the relief permitted under the statute. The Eleventh Circuit, for example, denied damages under Title IX. In an important Third Circuit case, however, the court held that compensatory damages were available for alleged violations of Title IX[46] if discriminatory intent on the part of the school board could be established.

The U.S. Supreme Court resolved the issue in its landmark 1992 decision, *Franklin v. Gwinnett County Public Schools*[47] by overruling the decision of the Eleventh Circuit. Franklin was a student at North Gwinnett High School in Gwinnett County, Georgia. She alleged that she was subjected to continual sexual harassment for a period of three years from her teacher, Andrew Hill, who was also a coach at the school. In her complaint she stated, among other things, that Hill forcibly kissed her on numerous occasions and coercively subjected her to sexual intercourse. She also alleged that the school was aware of her charges and that they investigated the complaints, but took no action against Hill. She also claimed that they discouraged her from pressing charges against him. Hill later resigned on the condition that all matters pending against him be dropped, and the school subsequently closed its investigation.

Before bringing her lawsuit, Franklin filed a complaint with the Office for Civil Rights. They investigated the charges for several months and concluded that the school district had violated Franklin's rights by subjecting her to physical and verbal sexual harassment and by interfering with her right to complain about conduct proscribed by Title IX. However, OCR dropped its investigation when it determined that the school district had come into compliance with Title IX since it had adopted a grievance procedure and since Hill had resigned. Franklin's subsequent lawsuit was also dismissed because the court ruled that the statute did not authorize an award of damages and that the matter was moot. The case was appealed and eventually reached the United States Supreme Court.

The Supreme Court drew a parallel between a supervisor who sexually harasses a subordinate because of the subordinate's sex and a teacher who harasses a student because of the student's sex. Because the employer has a duty not to discriminate on the basis of sex, the Supreme Court stated: "We believe the same rule should apply when a teacher sexually harasses and abuses a student. Congress surely did not intend for federal monies to be expended to support the intentional actions it sought by statute to proscribe."[48] The Court concluded that a damages remedy is available for an action brought to enforce Title IX. The case has been sent back to the lower court to determine if an award of damages is warranted in this case, and if so, how much should be awarded.

Title IX is analogous to Title VII. It tends to track the caselaw as it develops under Title VII and provides that sexual harassment is a form of discrimination on the basis of sex. In either a work or a school setting, one in authority may often use a superior role to force a member of the opposite sex to comply with demands. In both cases, the victim is denied the benefits of working or receiving an education in an environment free of discrimination. Just as the employer is held responsible for sex discrimination in the workplace, the school district will be held accountable for sex discrimination on the school campus. By analogy, a *quid pro quo* case can occur in a school as readily as in an office--a teacher's exchange of grades, favorable recommendations to college, or other benefits, for sexual favors. Similarly, hostile environment claims can occur and do occur even more often in the school environment than on the job. The potential for sexual harassment, primarily by peers, in the classrooms, in the gym, in the cafeteria, in the auditorium, in the halls, in the laboratories, on the buses, and on the athletic field is almost limitless.

In a hostile environment case, as in a *quid pro quo* case, students discriminated against are denied the benefits of the equal education mandated by Title IX. Those damages available to a student harassed by a teacher may also be available to a student sexually harassed by another student when the harassment is so severe or pervasive as to create the hostile environment. If the school knows or should have known that a hostile environment has been created in the school, and if that school takes no action to remedy the hostile environment, it can be held liable for monetary damages. In addition to the remedies of injunctive relief; reinstatement; back pay; compensatory and punitive damages, attorneys' fees, and costs provided under Title IX, a school district may also be held liable for additional penalties under state statute or federal law. Additional liability can be incurred by a school district should a student or school employee sue the district under other state or federal statutes.

Other recent, widely-publicized cases, some of which have implicated Title IX, have also drawn attention to sexual harassment in the schools and have resulted in changes in those school districts where the alleged harassment occurred. Most cases were settled out of court. Ironically, the school districts involved in the first two cases had sex discrimination policies in place before the harassment took place.

In the first case, a female student at Central High in Duluth, Minnesota, was the victim of obscene graffiti scrawled on the walls of the boys' bathroom. Even after she and her family complained to the school, the graffiti continued for the next eighteen months. The graffiti was not removed until a school district ordered a janitor to scrub the walls in August, 1989. By that time, the family had requested help sixteen times. The student then filed a complaint with the Minnesota Department of Human Rights. She charged that her school district had violated the Minnesota Human Rights Act, which prohibits sexual harassment. She alleged that the school had done nothing to stop the graffiti and had allowed an environment of sexual harassment to flourish that interfered with her education. In September, 1991, the commission found that the school should have done more to put a stop to the graffiti. The Duluth school system has agreed to pay the victim $15,000. The school system has also revised its sexual harassment policy, now provides training for students and staff, and checks the bathrooms daily for graffiti.

A similar suit was filed against a school district in Chaska, a suburb of Minneapolis. A female student, alleging violation of the Minnesota Human Rights Act, complained about lewd jokes and obscene skits at pep rallies, a student who used a centerfold as a book cover, and a circulating list of the twenty-five most "fuckable" girls. The list also included graphic descriptions of the girls' bodies. The Minnesota Department of Human Rights found that the school district responded inappropriately to incidents of sexual harassment, thereby creating an "offensive atmosphere that promotes sexual harassment in general." District officials were ordered to go through conciliation counseling with the student. At the conciliation stage, the state commission attempts to determine the wishes of the victim, which, if reasonable, are then conveyed to the school. Ideally, a settlement mutually agreeable to both sides is reached. Among other things, a settlement may involve a monetary penalty, policy changes in the school district, or counseling of the offender(s).

More recently, a second-grade female in the Eden Prairie school district in suburban Minneapolis filed a related complaint with the state Human Rights Department and with the U.S. Department of Education. The student's mother complained that her daughter was forced to endure teasing, foul language and lewd behavior from the boys on her school bus. She argued that the steps taken by the school to remedy the sexually harassing behavior were insufficient. That case, as of this writing, is still pending.

In another recent case, a female student in Petaluma, California, was subjected to lines of her classmates mooing at her throughout the school day as well as before and after school. When she complained, her teacher told her she would "just have to put up with it." The mooing continued through high school. Despite complaints from the girl's parents to school officials, the sexually harassing behavior continued. The parents then filed a Title IX suit with OCR. OCR found that the school district had failed to appropriately address the problem, and the student sued her school district, alleging emotional distress. The case was settled out of court for $20,000.

Although the amount of money for which the victims settled in these cases may seem small, the potential for large numbers of suits by students and resulting damages is great. Should the school district have to pay to settle many suits or litigate them in court, the total cost to the district--in resources and in adverse publicity--could be considerable.

The discussions of the preceding cases suggest that complaints about sexual harassment by students will most likely increase and that complainants are getting younger. As students and school employees become more aware of the statutes covering sexual harassment, they will tolerate harassment less and demand that schools do more to stop it. Many advocates of reform believe that a step toward eliminating sexual harassment and reducing school district liability is for each state to pass a statute mandating that every school district have a policy on sexual harassment. For an example of one state statute, see the Appendix.

Other Applicable Statutes
Federal Law: Section 1983

Another federal statute available to both students and employees is the Civil Rights Act of 1871, 42 U.S.C. Section 1983, commonly referred to as Section 1983. A complainant might prefer to use this law rather than Title VII or Title IX (or in addition to it) since it provides the right to a jury trial, the potential for increased awards for damages, and speedier access to the courts because administrative channels need not be exhausted prior to filing suit. A cautionary note is that the statute may be inapplicable to state universities protected by the Eleventh Amendment, which prohibits citizens from suing their states. Section 1983 authorizes lawsuits by public school students and employees against "governmental officials" for violations of federal constitutional and statutory law. The law is inapplicable to private institutions, but may be used by those who were denied the federal rights listed below by persons who were acting "under color of" state law. A "person" under section 1983 is usually limited to employees of state or local governments who are sued in their individual capacities. The official misuses power conferred on him by state law; generally, that means that he commits the infraction while he is performing the duties of the job he was employed to do. The law is more likely to apply to supervisors than to co-workers.

The federal rights most commonly raised are the Fourteenth Amendment, the First Amendment, and federal statutes. In the context of discrimination based on sex, the equal protection clause of the Fourteenth Amendment protects a victim from gender discrimination that is intentional. The due process clause of that Amendment protects a claimant from being deprived of "property" or "liberty" without due process of law. A property interest might be a right in continued employment, such as that guaranteed by a one-year or a five-year contract.

Liberty interests can be reputational interests. An employee who complains of sexual harassment and is fired by a supervisor who then defames the employee, has deprived the employee of a liberty interest. He has harmed her reputation. A second liberty interest is in privacy; that is, in keeping personal matters confidential.

Another, more literal, liberty interest is the freedom from physical restraint. In *Stoneking v. Bradford Area School District*[49], a former student brought suit against the school district, the principal, assistant principal, and the superintendent for failing to take action to protect the "health, safety and welfare of the female student body" from the alleged sexual harassment and abuse of the band director, Edward Wright. Stoneking charged the defendants maintained a policy of "reckless indifference to instances of known or suspected sexual abuse of students by teachers." The court held that Stoneking could sustain a Section 1983 action due to the defendants' maintaining a "policy, practice or custom which directly caused her constitutional harm." She alleged she was deprived of her liberty interest in being free from "invasion of her personal security through sexual abuse." This decision enabled Stoneking to sue the school district and individual school officials for negligent supervision of Wright. The significance of the case is that it established that, under certain conditions, liability can now be shifted from the sexual harasser to the school district and its officials.

The court will look to two key factors in determining whether the school district will be held liable for the acts of its employees. First, the frequency of the sexual conduct is significant. The more incidents of sexual harassment there are, the more likely it is that a school district will be held liable. Second, the school's response to the incidents will be considered. The promptness and appropriateness of administrators' actions after they have been informed of the harassment will help determine the school's liability.

It is important to note, however, that Section 1983 has limited application. A recent case in the same circuit as *Stoneking* distinguished between the culpability of school districts for sexual abuse by a "state actor" in contrast to sexual abuse by fellow students.[50] In that case, the female plaintiffs, D.R., a minor, and another student, attended Middle Bucks Area Vocational Technical School where they were enrolled in a graphic arts class. While attending the arts class, the girls contended they were sexually molested by seven male students in the unisex bathroom and darkroom that were part of their graphic arts classroom. They alleged their sexual assaults occurred two to four times a week over a five-month period during class. The Section 1983 suit was brought against school administrators, a student teacher in charge of the graphic arts class, and two guidance counselors, alleging they knew or should have known of the abuse. In affirming the District Court, which had dismissed the suit, the Circuit Court stated that this case lacked the "linchpin" of *Stoneking*. Because "private actors"--the students--had committed the violations, not "state actors"-- school personnel--neither the school nor its employees could be held liable under Section 1983.

The First Amendment may also be invoked under Section 1983. For example, a school district that retaliates against an employee who complains of sexual harassment violates the First

Amendment rights of the employee. More commonly, the First Amendment is implicated when a teacher is repressed for speaking out about a public issue, such as a political candidate. He may then file a Section 1983 suit against the school district.

Section 1983 may also be used to enforce federal statutory law. Titles VII and IX are examples of two laws that could be enforced by Section 1983. Before damages were available under Title VII by statute and under Title IX by ruling of the Supreme Court, Section 1983 was commonly used in some circuits. Other circuits, however, refused to permit it to be invoked against state schools.

Under Section 1983 school officials may be sued in their individual as well as in their official capacities. Furthermore, they may be liable for the harassing conduct of their subordinates if it can be shown that they condoned, encouraged, or were indifferent to their subordinate's actions. An important aspect on which a case may turn is whether the official had notice of the sexually harassing behavior. Having notice is more than having firsthand experience. It also includes being forewarned about those behaviors that the official "should have known" about. For example, phone calls and letters from parents complaining that a teacher is making improper advances to students should put the principal of a school on notice that she needs to investigate the complaints. She is not permitted to ignore complaints and then claim she didn't know about the teacher's behavior.

A wide range of damages is available to claimants under section 1983. They include nominal, compensatory, and punitive damages. Under compensatory damages are included those for emotional distress and for damage to reputation as well as for humiliation. Although municipalities are immune from punitive damages, supervisors acting either in their official or individual capacity are not. They can be held personally accountable for reckless indifference to the federal rights of a plaintiff.

State Law: Employment-Related Law
Fair Employment Practices (FEP) Statutes

All states have statutes similar to Title VII that prohibit discrimination in employment. Most statutes also create administrative agencies to insure that these laws are enforced. The administrative agencies are typically called the Human Rights Commission or the Civil Rights Commission. However, state employment laws may differ significantly from Title VII, and their provisions vary from state to state. For example, some FEP agencies have the authority to force employers to submit to an administrative hearing. If the employer is found liable at that hearing, the FEP can enforce an award of damages. In some states, the FEP administrative remedies must be exhausted before a plaintiff may use the court system, and, as with the EEOC, the agency must issue a right-to-sue letter. Most often the EEOC and the FEP agencies work together to avoid duplication of services and to coordinate their investigative procedures.

The majority of states have FEP agencies that are "designated" by the EEOC. Among the designated agencies, most have dual-filing agreements with the EEOC. This means that a filing with the state agency automatically effects a filing with the EEOC, and vice versa. The significance of dual-filing is that the complainant gets whatever benefits are available under either law.

Remedies under FEP laws are not consistent among the states. Some FEP statutes provide for compensatory and punitive damages; others permit only compensatory damages. Still other statutes do not authorize agencies to award either compensatory or punitive damages. In those states that provide monetary damages, the amount allowed may exceed that provided by Title VII. Another important aspect of FEP statutes is that in some states if an FEP agency has heard a case and has made a judicial decision, a plaintiff may later be foreclosed from trying that case in a federal court. It is wise to be familiar with individual state FEP laws and to keep abreast of any changes in the laws.

Workers' Compensation

Workers' compensation statutes are intended to compensate employees for work-related injuries without regard to fault. Employees who are injured on the job can settle a claim quickly but only for a limited amount. Employers pay a monthly sum for each employee into a general fund. Although some states permit actions against an employer for sexual harassment under the Workers' Compensation statute, the same statutes may also provide that this is the exclusive remedy for the injury. Thus, other state law remedies normally available to a plaintiff, such as invasion of privacy, might be barred. A defendant will usually argue that any plaintiff pursuing a sexual harassment complaint under a Workers' Compensation statute should be prohibited from advancing any other claim. Some courts, however, have held that workplace injuries brought about due to sexual harassment are outside the scope of Worker's Compensation laws.

Under Workers' Compensation statutes the employee must suffer a disability or need for medical attention. Emotional distress, therefore, may not be covered under such a claim unless there are physical manifestations. The injury must also be sufficiently work-related to be actionable. Additionally, some states limit coverage to injuries that are accidental.

Remedies available under Workers' Compensation statutes are limited to 1) an award of past and future medical care, 2) a percentage of salary lost during a period of recuperation from the injury, and 3) a settlement for permanent disability resulting in lost earning capacity.

Unemployment Compensation

Sexual harassment often leads to unemployment: of either the victim, the harasser, or both. Under usual conditions, a worker who voluntarily quits her job, absent good cause, is not eligible for unemployment compensation. In some states, "good cause" has included sexual harassment proscribed by Title VII. The severity of the harassment may be a significant factor in these cases. Some courts have also held that claimants must first follow the grievance procedures provided by their employers before they can be request unemployment compensation. However, in cases where reporting the offense may have been futile, courts may allow the claim. There must be a direct link between the employee's voluntary termination and the sexual harassment; that is, the harassment must be the "real reason" for the resignation.

Unemployment compensation claims are handled by administrative agencies, and judicial review of their decisions is limited. One crucial issue in unemployment compensation cases is whether a decision by the administrative agency will prevent the plaintiff from relitigating the same issue in a separate court action. If the claim was heard by an agency acting in a judicial capacity and all parties had a full and fair opportunity to be heard, a plaintiff may find that she cannot try these issues in any subsequent proceeding.

Wrongful Discharge

Although many states still claim that employees may be fired at the will of their employer (for cause or for no cause at all), an increasing number of states now recognize that employees may not be fired for refusing to tolerate conduct that violates public policy. For example, no employee is expected to tolerate sexual harassment. The concept behind the claim is that employees are not required to commit an act that the public would denounce. Some courts reject wrongful discharge claims and insist that the state FEP statute is the plaintiff's exclusive statelaw remedy. Other courts have permitted wrongful discharge claims regardless of the availability of other claims.

Interference with a Contract

An employee sexually harassed by a co-worker or supervisor who can show that the harasser interfered with her performance of her employment contract may have a complaint against her co-worker or supervisor for wrongful interference with contract. This type of case is not instituted against the employer. The co-worker persuades the employer to retaliate against the female worker. She must show that she was prejudiced by the actions; for example, that she was fired or denied a promotion. The plaintiff must also show that the harasser intended to interfere with the employment relationship. A plaintiff who wins her case may be awarded compensatory damages. In addition, the plaintiff may be able to get punitive damages if she can prove her co-worker acted maliciously. In a New Jersey case based on Title VII and on tortious interference with an employment contract,[51] a federal court found five of the plaintiff's male co-workers and supervisors liable. The co-workers had made loud, sexually explicit remarks about the plaintiff and left an obscene and humiliating cartoon on her desk. Despite her complaints, her supervisors had failed to put a stop to the conduct, thereby interfering with her employment contract.

State Law--The Common Law: Civil Actions

The previously discussed statutes provide an employee with a remedy, but they restrict the damages that may be awarded and the time period during which a claim may be filed. For some claims a jury trial is not available. The following theories of recovery, available to students as well as to employees, may provide a more generous recovery and a more liberal time period in which to file a case.

The term "common law" describes all the laws and customs that were not created through enactments by legislatures. These laws and customs were derived from usage or from court decrees. The term "tort" is sometimes used to refer to these civil wrongs. Today, most of the common law has been codified, that is, state and municipal legislative bodies have passed statutes encompassing the common law and systematically organizing it. Common law claims potentially provide much greater amounts of money for either physical or emotional harm. Single or multiple common law claims may be filed, and they may be joined with Title VII or Title IX claims. Note that these statutes vary appreciably from state to state. The following is a general description of the applicable torts.

Assault and Battery

Assault and battery are usually asserted together, although they actually consist of two separate injuries. *Assault* is an attempt to cause physical contact coupled with the victim's fear that the contact was about to occur. Words alone are insufficient for the commission of this act.

> EXAMPLE: A student attempts to kiss another student but is thwarted by the intended victim who sidesteps the harasser.

Battery is an intended, completed, offensive physical contact. No mental or physical harm needs to have resulted and the touching can be with anything in contact with the plaintiff's body, such as a plate in her hand.

> EXAMPLE: The student completes the unwanted kiss.

Intentional Infliction of Emotional Distress (Outrage)

Intentional infliction of emotional distress is the most litigated common-law theory of recovery in sexual harassment cases. It is also one of the most difficult to prove since there is no precise definition of what constitutes outrageous conduct. The victim must prove: 1) the harasser behaved outrageously, 2) the harasser intended to cause or knew his behavior was likely to cause emotional distress, 3) the victim actually suffered emotional distress, and 4) the harasser's conduct actually caused the emotional distress. The victim is more likely to be successful in winning her case if she can show that she suffered physically as a result of her harassment or that she faced threats of retaliation for complaining. Verbal harassment alone is probably insufficient to win a case.

> EXAMPLE: A co-worker secures a print of a fellow employee nude and circulates it throughout the office where it is seen by administrators and students who enter the office.

False Imprisonment

False imprisonment is a tort in which 1) the harasser intentionally confines the victim within boundaries that he has fixed and 2) the victim is aware of the confinement.

> EXAMPLE: A student, larger than his victim, pins her up against a locker by placing his forearms on either side of her head. In this example, the student need not touch the victim, and the length of time of confinement is irrelevant. Even a few seconds may be sufficient for false imprisonment.

Invasion of Privacy

Invasion of privacy is most commonly an intrusion upon the "seclusion" of a victim. The intrusion must be offensive and encroach upon a truly private place or matter. Naturally, if the complainant herself freely discusses private, personal matters, such as her sexual experiences, she cannot make this claim.

> EXAMPLE: A boy follows a girl who has rejected him into the girls' restroom.
>
> EXAMPLE: A teacher persistently asks a student about her sex life with her boyfriend and "how far she has gone."

Defamation

Defamation may take two forms: if the defamation is written, the tort is libel; if it is oral, it is slander. The plaintiff must show that the defendant 1) made a false or damaging statement about the plaintiff, 2) communicated the statement to a third person, 3) deliberately or negligently communicated the statement, and 4) harmed the plaintiff in some way by making the statement. No proof of special harm is needed for libel. Special harm involves money losses, such as loss of a job or credit. For slander, proof of special harm is needed unless the slander involves: 1) the plaintiff's business, 2) the commission of a crime by the plaintiff, 3) a female plaintiff's lack of chastity, or 4) the plaintiff's contracting a loathsome disease.

> EXAMPLE: A student spreads a false rumor that a male teacher has been having sexual intercourse with a 14-year-old female student.
> EXAMPLE: Students circulate "slam books." On each page a girl's name appears and other students write in comments about the girl--her physical features, her sexual behavior with boys.
> EXAMPLE: Graffiti is written on the boys' restroom walls about sexual acts committed by a female student in the school.

Negligent Hiring, Retention, or Supervision

In claims of negligent hiring, retention, or supervision the plaintiff attempts to hold the employer liable for the sexually harassing acts of its employees. Her claim is that the employer knew or should have known of the employee's inclination to harass and failed to take appropriate action to protect his workers against it. By analogy, a teacher may be considered a supervisor under Title IX. The school in which he teaches may incur liability for his acts of sexual harassment against a student if the school knew or should have known of the teacher's propensities. A school that investigated charges of a teacher's acts of sexual harassment but failed to discharge the teacher because the investigators did not determine that his misconduct was sufficiently injurious may face serious liability should that teacher subsequently engage in more harmful conduct.

The preceding list of civil actions is not exhaustive, but includes those claims most frequently used in sexual harassment cases. Additionally, state civil rights acts, state constitutional law, and other state and local laws may form the basis of a claim. Most likely, if litigation results, an attorney will file multiple claims in a complaint. That way, should one claim fail, the plaintiff will have alternate theories on which to proceed. In summary, because different theories have different requirements and provide different forms of relief, the plaintiff will state her claim only after considering the following factors:

1) The nature of the injury and the extent of the harm
2) The statute of limitations imposed by each law
3) The remedy sought--whether injunction, job reinstatement, back pay, policy changes on the party of the employer, or monetary damages
4) If damages are sought, how much the plaintiff is asking for
5) The amount of time the plaintiff has--whether she can wait years for a decision or must have a settlement now
6) The number of employees in the school district
7) The status of the victim, whether student or employee
8) The likelihood of success on the claim
9) The expenses entailed by the remedy sought
10) The effect that publicity will have on the victim and on the school district
11) Whether the plaintiff who has an administrative hearing will be able to further litigate her claim
12) Whether the plaintiff wants a jury trial

Criminal Law

In addition to being liable in a civil action, sexual harassers, in some circumstances, may be charged with violations of criminal law. Reports are sometimes made by the victims, their families, physicians, and counselors, but that is not the only way cases are referred to the police. In most states school staff members, among others, have a statutory obligation to report suspected cases of child abuse to the authorities, typically to a social services agency. This agency may refer the case to the appropriate law enforcement agency.

The criminal law is punitive and serves to deter others from committing similar crimes. Penalties range from imprisonment to fines, community service, and restitution. Resulting damage to the reputation of those convicted can foreclose future job opportunities and result in stigma in the community. The following is a list of potential charges that may be filed against sexual harassers.

Criminal Sexual Conduct (Rape)

Most statutes define rape as non-consensual sexual intercourse in which the offender uses physical force, the threat of a deadly weapon, or intimidation to effect physical penetration.

Statutory Rape

Regardless whether the victim consents, if sexual intercourse is accomplished with a female under the statutory age of consent (typically, sixteen or eighteen), the crime of statutory rape has been committed.

Deviant Sexual Intercourse (Sodomy)

This crime includes oral or anal sex or any form of intercourse with an animal.

Sexual Battery/Sexual Assault

Non-consensual contact with an intimate part of the body (including contact through clothing) is sexual battery. Intimate parts of the body include the breasts, sexual organs, buttocks, anus, and groin. The charge may be joined with false imprisonment (see below).

If the sexual battery is incomplete, the defendant may be charged with sexual assault. He may also be charged with attempted rape and battery.

Indecent Exposure

Exposure of the genitals with knowledge that the conduct will likely cause affront or alarm is indecent exposure.

Obscene Telephone Calls

Federal law is implicated in this crime which prohibits obscene or harassing telephone calls. Prohibitions include making lewd comments and annoying, repetitive, or threatening phonecalls.

False Imprisonment

This crime is the same as its civil counterpart (above). It is the deprivation of another's liberty within specified bounds and against her will. It is usually accompanied by other charges, such as rape.

It is important for a defendant charged with a sexual harassment-related crime to remember that the standard for his conviction is that he must be proved guilty "beyond a reasonable doubt." However, the school district is not bound by the decision of a judge or jury in a criminal trial *even if the defendant is acquitted of the crime.* If, after its own investigation, the school finds that under a lesser standard than "beyond a reasonable doubt" the charges are substantiated, even a permanent teacher may be dismissed. Information provided to the police or other agencies will also be available to the school. Statutory criteria that provide for teacher dismissal in most states are, typically, "immorality" or other "neglect of duty."

Another point to keep in mind is that the offense need not occur on school grounds to be actionable. A teacher who invites a minor student to his apartment where he attempts to engage her in sexual intercourse can be charged with a crime just as though the behavior had occurred at school. While the charge is pending against him, he will normally be suspended, probably with pay.

Employers may also face criminal liability for the acts of their harassing employees if they aided or encouraged the defendant. They may be charged if they conceal a crime or are accessories after the fact of a sexual harassment-related crime. For example, a school district that transfers a teacher who has committed a crime to another school to help him evade prosecution may be charged with being an accessory after the fact.

Common Employer Defenses Which Frequently Fail[52]

Employers may feel they are protected if they did not know about instances of sexual harassment in their schools or if they had a policy prohibiting sexual discrimination that was ignored by an employee. When a law suit is brought, they may find that they are liable regardless whether they knew sexual harassment was occurring and regardless whether they had a policy in effect. The Minnesota School Boards Association lists defenses that are often argued by school districts but which frequently fail:

1. *The employer did not know about the harassment.* Lack of knowledge will not insulate the employer in cases of sexual harassment by a supervisor. The employer will be held strictly liable in cases of *quid pro quo* harassment. In cases of hostile environment harassment, the employer may still be held liable if he should have known about the harassment or if he took no steps to promptly remediate an occurrence of sexual harassment.

2. *The harassed employee did not report the harassment or did not follow established procedures.* This defense may fail if:
   a. the harassment was reported by another employee;
   b. the harassed employee was afraid to report it;
   c. the employer did not have a policy;
   d. the employer did not effectively communicate its policy.

3. *The employer investigated and took action.* This defense may fail if the investigation is not thorough, complete,

and impartial, or if the action taken against the harasser is too lenient or inappropriate.

4. *The harassed employee voluntarily participated.* The standard for determining whether sexual harassment exists is whether the sexual advances were welcome not whether they were voluntary. If the employee was coerced or pressured into submitting to the sexual advances--even though her actions were voluntary--if the advances were unwelcome, the employer may still be held liable.

5. *The harassed employee suffered no damages.* The employer may be liable even if the employment status of the harassed employee was not adversely affected. Although the employee may not have been fired or denied a pay raise, the school district may still be liable for compensatory and punitive damages if it "intentionally" discriminated or if it was recklessly indifferent to its employee's rights. It may also be liable if the employee suffered mental distress or other non-monetary losses.

6. *The harassed employee quits.* If the reason the employee quit was sexual harassment, she has been constructively discharged, and the employer may not be able to use her leaving her job as a defense.

The Role of Labor Unions and Arbitration in Sexual Harrassment Cases

In many states, where the majority of teachers are represented by a union, significant factors to consider are the collective bargaining agreement and the role of arbitration in a case of sexual harassment. Standards of appropriate workplace conduct under Title VII have been incorporated into most collective bargaining agreements. Anti-discrimination clauses protect union members from sexual harassment whether that particular term is used. Sexually harassed workers usually report their grievance to a union steward. Most likely, the worker will then have the option of following the union's established grievance procedure. Next, through meetings with the employer, the harasser, the victim, and the union arbitrator, the arbitrator will attempt to effectively halt the harassment and to punish the harasser. The American Federation of State, County, and Municipal Employees (AFSCME) has published a booklet, *Sexual Harassment: What the Union Can Do*, that provides information on recent court decisions, conducting a sample survey on sexual harassment in the workplace, contract language, policy statements, and other law-related issues. (See Appendix for ordering information.)

It is important to note that the courts and union procedures may not be mutually exclusive. A union-represented complainant may pursue union arbitration and a civil suit against her employer simultaneously. However, most claims of sexual harassment are litigated in court rather than submitted to arbitration. In the majority of arbitrated sexual harassment cases, the grievance is filed by a union-represented defendant who has been fired or otherwise disciplined. The exclusive remedy, for disciplined employees, is limited to the grievance and arbitration procedure. That is, the results of arbitration are final and may not be appealed in a court of law.

In states where teachers are union members, complaints of possible sexual misconduct on the part of a teacher must be handled by following the complaint procedure specified in the collective bargaining agreement. There may be procedural requirements that administrators must comply with, such as notification of the teacher against whom charges are alleged within a five- or ten-day deadline. Under some collective bargaining agreements, suspension of teachers may be limited to five days before the district must reinstate or begin dismissal proceedings against him. Districts that fail to follow these procedures may be prohibited from using the information gathered from a complainant in a later disciplinary action against the teacher.

Whether a sexually harassed complainant files a grievance under the collective bargaining agreement, she may still bring a sexual harassment civil action against her employer. That action, however, must be based on legal principles, such as the public policy against discrimination in employment. The legal principle must be applied apart from any analysis under the terms of the collective bargaining agreement. Should she file a legitimate grievance following union procedure, under the National Labor Relations Act, the union must fairly represent her or it can be liable for damages. Fair representation means that the union's conduct toward its grieving member is not arbitrary, discriminatory, or in bad faith. Of course, the union itself is bound to the discriminatory policies proscribed by Title VII and is subject to the same type of suits as a school district. If the union steward refuses to handle the union member's complaint of sexual harassment, the employee has the right to appeal. Furthermore, the employee who has followed the grievance procedure and who is dissatisfied with the results may take her case to the EEOC or to the state FEP agency.

Although the employee alleging sexual harassment may appeal her case, an employee disciplined under the grievance and arbitration regulations of a collective bargaining agreement is restricted to that remedy. Note that he may still have criminal and civil charges brought against him in separate proceedings. Furthermore, under a collective bargaining agreement, unless the arbitrator exceeded his authority by deciding an issue outside the employment contract, the decision of the arbitrator may not be appealed to the courts. A limited exception may be for those cases in which the decision is contrary to public policy. However, some courts have held that the arbitration award must violate the law before they will vacate it.

Where Does the First Amendment Fit In?

School districts have a number of defenses available when charged with sexual discrimination. For example, they may argue that sexual harassment never occurred, that if harassment did occur they had no notice of it, that the statute of limitations for the claim has expired, or that the complainant has not availed herself of the grievance procedure provided by the school district. Seldom raised in litigated cases, however, is a First Amendment defense: that sexually harassing speech is protected by the United States Constitution. Until courts address this issue, it is unclear to what extent verbally harassing speech is protected.

At issue is that portion of the First Amendment that reads, "Congress shall make no law. . . abridging the freedom of speech." (U.S. Const. amend. I) In the context of the school setting, does the First Amendment afford students and other school personnel a Constitutional right to use sexually explicit language even though listeners may be intimidated or offended by it? Can a student paper his locker with pinups and pornographic drawings and still claim the First Amendment for protection?

For employees alleging *quid pro quo* harassment, the issue is clearer than for hostile environment harassment. Obviously, not all speech is protected. In the classic example, freedom of speech does not entitle a patron in a crowded theater to yell, "Fire!" with impunity when no fire exists. Freedom of speech protects neither the obscene nor the defamatory. The First Amendment will not shield child pornographers or perjurers. Threats to harm another or to extort "payment" for acts done or not done are not protected forms of speech. Therefore, threats, such as those to fire an employee who refuses to submit to sexual advances, are also not protected.

Sexual speech that interferes with a person's work or learning environment so that an intimidating or offensive environment is created is more troublesome. The U.S. Constitution offers broad protection for speech, regardless of the age of the speaker. As former Supreme Court Justice Fortas noted in a case involving students who protested the government's policy in Viet Nam by wearing black armbands, "It can hardly be argued that either students or teachers shed their constitutional rights to freedom of speech or expression at the schoolhouse gate."[53] To what extent, however, the First Amendment will shield students and school personnel in hostile environment cases is unsettled.

One case in which a First Amendment defense has been raised involved a woman employed as a welder in a Florida shipyard. In the *Jacksonville Shipyards* case, women employees were subjected not only to offensive oral comments but also to offen-sive pictures, calendars, photographs, and drawings. Defendants argued this "speech" was Constitutionally protected. The court denied the First Amendment defense. District Judge Melton reasoned:

1) The employees, not the employer, intended to express themselves. Therefore, the employer could insist on an end to the posting of pinups and other damaging materials without abridging employees' free speech rights.
2) The pictures and verbal harassment of the women employees were not "protected" because they acted as discriminatory "conduct," rather than speech. The court likened this form of "speech" to threats of violence or blackmail, which are also not protected.
3) Regulation of discriminatory speech in the workplace is only time, place, and manner regulation. These regulations on speech have traditionally been upheld.
4) The women workers were a captive audience for the men who spoke to them and ridiculed them. Had the women been able to look away and avoid the pictures and comments, the speech might not have been considered discriminatory.
5) The First Amendment rights of the male workers must be balanced against the right of the female workers to work in a non-discriminatory atmosphere. Since the government's interest in achieving equality in the workplace is "compelling" and the regulation is narrowly drawn to attain this interest, the regulations are permissible.
6) Drawing a parallel to public employee speech cases, the court stated that just as an employer may discharge an employee whose exercise of free expression undermines the workforce, the employer may also curtail the free expression of employees in order to remedy the demonstrated harm inflicted on other employees and proscribed by the government. In either case, the First Amendment is not violated.
7) The harm being perpetrated is on identifiable individuals, and it was not directed at women in general.

Those who oppose the curb on speech in hostile environment cases claim that silencing the speakers, regardless of the offensiveness of their remarks, is tantamount to the implementation of a speech code. During the past several years, universities imposing such a code have attempted to reduce incidents of "hate speech," which is based on race, gender, or ethnicity. These policies have repeatedly been struck down by federal courts as overly broad. In June, 1992, the Supreme Court invalidated a St. Paul Minnesota, statute prohibiting "bias-motivated crime."[54] The statute banned displays of a symbol (in effect, speech) which creates "anger, alarm, or resentment" in others based on race, color, creed, religion or gender. The Court held that the First Amendment prohibited St. Paul from banning only certain disfavored subjects of speech while permitting other abusive speech not addressed to those topics. Although the majority recognized a narrow exception for Title VII hostile environment "speech," four Justices challenged that exception and stated that following the Court's announced principle, "hostile work environment claims based on sexual harassment should fail First Amendment review."

Traditionally, restrictions on the First Amendment have been extremely narrow. It would be inconsistent and unconstitutional to afford college students First Amendment rights, yet deny those same rights to students in middle school or high school merely because they are younger.

On the other hand, the Supreme Court has from time-to-time called attention to the uniqueness of the school setting in which younger children may be found. In a case involving the search of a student's pocketbook by school administrators[55], Justice White noted the "substantial interest of teachers and administrators in maintaining discipline in the classroom and on school grounds."[56] In the same case the Court recognized the need to preserve order and a "proper educational environment [which requires] close supervision of schoolchildren, as well as the enforcement of rules against conduct that would be perfectly permissible if undertaken by an adult."[57] The Court noted that the school has an obligation to instruct children in the foundations of our government and its democratic processes. In recognition of these special needs and obligations, the Court has ac-knowledged that a greater flexibility must be accorded school personnel in administering their schools. In sum, the duties and obligations of school administrators must be balanced against the Constitutional rights of school children and teachers.

In both the workplace and in school, sexually harassing remarks directed at an individual will probably be afforded less First Amendment protection than those general sexual remarks overheard by a student on her way to class. The reasoning behind this is those comments addressed to an individual are much more likely to be perceived as threatening. As such, direct remarks have a greater potential to interfere with a person's performance in the workplace and a student's performance at school.

However, in many of the complaints against schools that have been filed with civil rights agencies today, none or only some of the offensive speech is being directed against specific students. Two issues are raised by these complaints: 1) How severe and pervasive must the sexual speech be in order for a hostile environment to be created? and 2) How significant will it be that students are captive audiences, unable to avoid the offensive speech in the halls, in the classrooms, and often off the school grounds? A student who must ride the bus provided by the school and who is confronted daily by the lewd comments, gender-demeaning remarks, and other offensive expressions by fellow bus-riders is part of a captive audience and may not merely turn away and refuse to hear. A student who must use a restroom covered with obscene graffiti or a female student demeaned by graffiti written about her on the walls in the boys' restroom confronts a hostile and abusive environment that can interfere with that student's learning in the classroom. Schools who refuse to deal with these problems after receiving numerous complaints from students and their parents are likely to face unpleasant and expensive lawsuits. They must also confront parents who are angry either because their children have been harmed or who are angry because taxpayers' money is being spent to settle these suits.

The federal courts have not yet heard a hostile environment suit involving a middle school or high school where the sexual harassment is severe and pervasive but not directed at an individual. If and when the courts do hear such cases, the defense of the First Amendment is likely to be raised. In light of that defense, the courts will consider numerous factors, some of which are unique to the school setting. Of primary importance will be the extent to which the ability of individual students to learn is being impeded by the sexually harassing speech. Related to this criterion is the extent to which the entire school is being disrupted. If students are unable to escape the harassment, the Court will consider what steps the school took to deal with the offensive language once they knew about it. Whether they had a policy informing students about sexual harassment, an accessible grievance procedure, and a means of carrying out their policy will be important. How quickly the school responded to complaints of harassment will also be a factor.

The court will consider the role of the school in the community. School personnel are responsible not only for the education of children but also for their protection. The options of adults in the workplace are different than those for children who, for the most part, are unable to switch schools or leave school entirely.

Another influential factor in determining whether the First Amendment will protect speech is the location of the speech. Is it in a place where "public discourse" usually occurs? Unlike a public park or sidewalk, the school will probably not qualify as an arena for public discourse. Therefore, less First Amendment protection will be afforded that location.

Finally, the court will consider the goals of Congress in enacting Title VII and Title IX. It may be argued that some forms of content-based discrimination are justified because they are narrowly tailored to serve compelling state interests. In this case the compelling state interest is equality of educational opportunity; therefore, the argument goes, the First Amendment may not protect pornography and other sexual harassment in the middle and secondary school setting.

3
What Steps Can the School Take To Prevent Sexual Harassment?

All school district personnel want to avoid liability for sexual harassment. The costs of condoning or tolerating sexual harassment are not just monetary. Damage to reputation and interference with the harasser's livelihood are likely. Community unrest, dissatisfaction, and distrust of the school system can result from accusations of harassment. The most and longest-lasting damage, however, is to the victims. The physical and psychological damage they suffer may be irreparable. High absenteeism, poor grades and work performance, and a large turnover in personnel often accompany sexual harassment.

Assessing the School District's Policy on Sexual Harassment

Although having a sound anti-discrimination policy will not necessarily protect a school district from liability, not having one will definitely increase the possibility that a school district will be held liable in cases of sexual harassment. For school districts with no policy or program geared toward eradicating sexual harassment or that question the adequacy of their program, the following checklist, adapted from one developed by the University of Michigan School of Education,[58] may be a starting point:

Is Sexual Harassment a Problem in Your School?

This checklist has been developed to assist school districts in assessing the level of effort they have expended to prevent sexual harassment from occurring and in determining the level of sexual harassment that actually occurs in their district. The checklist applies to sexual harassment of both students and staff.

Checklist: What Can You Do To Prevent Sexual Harassment In Your School?

To score the checklist, make a check mark next to each action that has been taken in your district, count the number of check marks, then, using the guide, see how your district rates.

1. Develop a specific policy against sexual harassment.
    ____Do you have such a policy?
    ____Has the policy been disseminated to staff?
    ____Has the policy been disseminated to students?
    ____Is there a procedure to inform new employees and students of the policy?

2. Develop a grievance procedure to handle complaints about sexual harassment. This may or may not be the same as other grievance procedures.
    ____Do you have such a grievance procedure?
    ____Has information about this procedure been disseminated to staff?
    ____Has information about this procedure been disseminated to students?

___Is there a similar grievance procedure written into any union contracts?

3. Develop a code of conduct for all employees, students and vendors.

    ___Is there any reference to sexual harassment in the student discipline code?

    ___Does the student handbook contain policy language regarding sexual harassment?

    ___Is there any reference to sexual harassment in the employee code of conduct?

    ___Does the employee handbook contain policy language regarding sexual harassment?

    ___Do union contracts and affirmative action plans for the district contain policy language regarding sexual harassment?

    ___Are student placement worksites notified of school sexual harassment policy?

4. Sensitize students and staff to the issue of sexual harassment to assure their understanding of the definition of sexual harassment, the laws regarding sexual harassment, and methods for dealing with complaints.

    ___Has there been a training program for district administration?

    ___Has there been a training program for district teachers, guidance counselors, and other employees including worksite supervisors?

    ___Has there been a training program for students?

    ___Has material on sexual harassment been included in courses on human relations or job skills?

    ___Can pamphlets advising students and staff about the nature of sexual harassment and its legal implications be found around the school?

    ___Has a school-wide conference or speakout been organized by students and/or staff to sensitize the school community to the issue of sexual harassment?

5. Reach out to populations of students who are known to be particularly vulnerable to sexual harassment.

    ___Have support groups been established for students enrolled in vocational or academic classes that are nontraditional for their gender?

    ___Are students who drop vocational or academic classes that are nontraditional for their gender routinely surveyed to establish the reason for dropping and to determine whether sexual harassment played any role in their decision to drop?

___Are student placement worksites regularly evaluated for evidence of sexual harassment?

Scoring the Checklist

16-21 points: Your district has obviously embarked upon a well-planned and determined effort to eliminate sexual harassment.

7-15 points: While there are efforts being made to prevent sexual harassment in your district, there are many areas where you need to supplement that effort.

0-6 points: It is necessary for your district to begin examining this issue from the standpoint of liability and to assess basic levels of awareness. It would be advisable to begin with district policy issues and to work up to basic awareness of the problem within the district. Set a specific goal for completion of the first phase of the effort. Consider obtaining some support or assistance from an outside agency.

A U.S. Department of Education publication, "Sexual Harassment in the Schools,"[59] provides advice to schools implementing a sexual harassment policy. The Department advises that administrators must be strong in their commitment to adopt and follow through on a sexual harassment policy. Multiple case managers should be designated to hear complaints, such as a teacher, a guidance counselor, and an administrator. Both male and female case managers should be appointed. Students can talk to the person with whom they feel most comfortable. Cases involving harassment of a student by an adult, such as a teacher, should immediately be referred to the chief administrator in the school. In such cases, districts may want to use a special investigator, such as the school district's attorney. These cases may also involve violations of the criminal law which can be grounds for the employee's dismissal.

Once a policy is adopted, it must be widely disseminated and accompanied by training and discussion for students, teachers, guidance counselors and administrators. Awareness of this form of discrimination increases the possibility of sexual harassment being identified early and stopped informally. "Preventive training is most effective when it places sexual harassment in the context of social problems and clarifies that the cause is neither the failures of a particular school nor the inabilities of specific individuals to handle interpersonal problems."[60] The presence or absence of sexual harassment should be incorporated into performance reviews of all staff members. Even if a school has a sexual harassment policy, refusal to inform employees and students of its existence or to enforce it can result in liability for the employer.

Ultimately, no school can guarantee its teachers or students that it can control the behavior of everyone in the school building. What school districts can do is reduce their own risk of incurring liability and send a message to all school personnel and students that sexual harassment will not be tolerated. The following suggestions can assist school districts in achieving those goals:

10 Steps to Prevent Sexual Harassment in the School
1) Establish a zero-toleration sexual harassment policy.
2) Disseminate that policy to staff, students, parents, and the community-at-large, including new students and employees.
3) Query staff and students to discover whether sexual harassment is being experienced by them in their schools and to what extent. Use these results to plan in-service meetings for staff and curriculum for students.
4) Educate staff and students on sexual harassment: inform them of conduct prohibited by law, the effects of harassment on the victim, and suggested ways that victims might initially deal with harassers.
5) Provide an accessible grievance procedure to insure ease and confidentiality in reporting cases of sexual harassment.
6) Investigate reported instances of sexual harassment immediately and appropriately.
7) Keep accurate and up-to-date records of complaints, investigations conducted, and actions taken.
8) Discipline staff and students who sexually harass others in a fair manner, depending on the seriousness and per-

vasiveness of the harassment. Discipline needs to be consistent among schools within the district.

9) Monitor cases of sexual harassment after they have been investigated to insure there is no repetition of the offensive behavior or retaliation toward the victim.

10) Observe the school facility on a daily basis and remove sexually harassing and defamatory graffiti, signs, and posters.

Establishing a Sexual Harassment Policy for Staff and Students

Strong administrative leadership is crucial to the implementation of a sexual harassment policy. Unless the administration takes sexual harassment seriously, it cannot be expected that staff or students will. All administrators and supervisors must be united in promoting the policy.

A clear policy puts employees on notice of behavior that will not be tolerated. For the person who is harassed, the policy provides a guide to what action may be taken to end the harassment. The majority of complainants are not attempting to get rich or to "stir up trouble." They want the harassment to stop. Law suits typically result when an employer does nothing or responds inadequately to allegations of sexual harassment. Attorney Barbara Kate Repa notes that about 90% of all sexual harassment complaints are resolved either through company grievance procedures or by confronting the harasser and informing him that his behavior is unwelcome.

A good sexual harassment policy defines the term sexual harassment and gives examples of the types of behavior prohibited. The policy against sexual harassment should not be merged into a blanket anti-discrimination policy. District officials who assume that everyone will know sexual harassment is included in a general statement that "Discrimination will not be tolerated" increase their liability unless they specifically use and define the term "sexual harassment." A good policy also describes the procedure that is to be followed in filing a grievance and offers names or positions of alternate personnel to whom complainants may report their grievance. The policy lists the penalties that may be incurred for harassing behavior and assures the complainant that the school will respect the confidentiality of all parties involved. It also contains a statement assuring victims there will be no retaliation for reporting sexual harassment abuses.

It is necessary that the policy be written since a written policy more easily and clearly informs both offenders and victims of the procedures and penalties for sexual harassment. Having the policy in writing has greater impact on the reader and underscores the gravity with which the school district regards sexual harassment. A written policy also enables the school district to present a defense should allegations of sexual harassment arise.

Policies must be periodically updated to keep up with changes in the law and in society. Circulating the policy annually and asking for input from employees can be helpful in keeping the policy up-to-date.

OCR suggests that schools ask the following questions when developing a sexual harassment grievance procedure:

__Is the grievance procedure flexible enough to accommodate the wide range of incidents of sexual harassment?

__Is the grievance procedure coordinated with other institutional grievance procedure systems?

__Can a student be accompanied by a friend or advisor throughout the complaint process?

__Does the grievance procedure provide an opportunity for informal consultation and, where appropriate, informal resolution before moving into formal procedures?

__After initial contact in the grievance procedure, does the complainant have:

   control over whether or not further institutional action will be taken; and an opportunity to participate in decision-making regarding the method for resolving the matter?

_Is the grievance procedure process credible to the constituency it is designed to serve?

_Are persons of authority, credibility and sensitivity involved in the grievance procedure process?

_Does the grievance procedure adhere to the Title IX regulations?

_Does the grievance procedure provide for independent and impartial investigation which produces persuasive findings based on:

thorough fact finding;

careful review; and

opportunity for appeal?

_Is every effort made to protect the confidentiality of the parties?

_Is the opportunity for reprisal and retaliation minimized?

_Does the grievance procedure provide prompt and equitable resolution of the complaint?

_Are there time frames in the grievance procedure by which a complaint should be investigated and resolved?

_Is a thorough yet timely remedy possible within the established timetable?

_Does the grievance procedure include appropriate remedy for the complainant and institutional corrective action where there is a finding of sexual harassment?

_Does the grievance procedure include provisions for quality control, tracking, record keeping and data retrieval?

Staff Policy

The employer's handbook, distributed to all school personnel annually, should contain a section with a clear statement of the school district's policy on sexual harassment and the procedure to follow when filing a grievance. A sample policy follows that can be modified to suit the school district:

Sample Sexual Harassment Policy and Procedure for Staff[61]

I. Sources of the Policy

Title VII of the Civil Rights Act of 1964 (amended 1991) prohibits discrimination because of race, color, religion, sex or national origin in all employment practices, including conditions of employment.

Title IX of the Education Amendments of 1972 prohibits discrimination on the basis of sex in any education program receiving federal funds.

(Additional state law may be added here.)

II. The Policy

    A. It is the policy of the _____ Public Schools to maintain a learning and working environment that is free from sexual harassment. No employee or student of the district shall be subjected to sexual harassment.

    B. It shall be a violation of this policy for any member of the _____ Public Schools staff to harass another staff member or student through conduct or communications of a sexual nature as defined in Section III. It shall also be a violation of this policy for students to harass staff members through conduct or communications of a sexual nature as defined in Section III. The school will also take reasonable steps to prevent sexual harassment by non-employees, such as independent contractors.

    C. Each administrator shall be responsible for promoting understanding and acceptance of, and assuring compliance with, state and federal laws and board policy and procedures governing sexual harassment within his or her school or office.

    D. Violations of this policy or procedure will be cause for disciplinary action.

III. Definition

    A. Sexual harassment means unwelcome sexual advances, requests for sexual favors and other verbal or physical conduct of a sexual nature when:

        1. submission to such conduct is made either explicitly or implicitly a term or condition of a person's employment or advancement or of a student's participation in school programs or activities;

        2. submission to or rejection of such conduct by an employee is used as the basis for decisions affecting the employee;

       3. such conduct has the purpose or effect of unreasonably inter-
fering with an employee's performance or creating an intimidating, hostile, or offensive work environment.
  B. Sexual harassment, as set forth in Section III-A may include, but is
not limited to the following:
       1. Sexual behavior: verbal harassment or abuse, in person or by
telephone; non-verbal suggestive pictures, sounds, or gestures;
pressure for sexual activity or dates; repeated remarks to a person, with sexual or demeaning implications; unwelcome touching, cornering or other physical contact; suggesting or demanding sexual involvement, accompanied by implied or explicit
threats concerning one's job.
       2. Gender-based behavior: referring to women as "foxes," "chicks,"
"broads"; making statements about women based on stereotypes, such as, "She couldn't teach Drivers Ed. You know how
women drive"; suggesting women are unable to perform certain
jobs because they lack necessary qualities: "She could never be
principal. How could she handle the athletic department?"
  C. Sexual harassment may be overt or subtle. Some behavior which is
appropriate in a social setting may not be appropriate in the workplace. But whatever form it takes, verbal, non-verbal or physical,
sexual harassment can be insulting and demeaning to the recipient
and will not be tolerated in the workplace.

IV. Procedures
  A. Any person who alleges sexual harassment by a staff member or student in the school district may use the procedure detailed in the
_____ District Grievance Procedure or may complain directly to
his or her immediate supervisor, building principal, or district Title
IX Coordinator. Initial investigations of complaints will begin within
48 hours.
  B. The right to confidentiality, both of the complainant and of the
accused, will be respected consistent with the school district's legal
obligations, and with the necessity to investigate allegations of misconduct and to take corrective action when this conduct has
occurred.

V. Retaliation
Filing of a grievance or otherwise reporting sexual harassment will not
reflect upon the individual's status nor will it affect future employment or
work assignments. Complaints of retaliation will be investigated and
meritorious complaints will be punished.

VI. Sanctions
  A. A substantiated charge against a staff member in the school district shall subject such staff member to disciplinary action, including warnings, reprimands, suspension, or dismissal. A harasser may also be held legally liable under federal and state anti-discrimination laws and under the criminal laws of this state.
  B. A substantiated charge against a student in the school district shall subject that student to disciplinary action which may include reprimands, detention, suspension or expulsion, consistent with the student discipline code. A harasser may also be held legally liable under state civil and criminal law.

VII. Notifications
  Notice of this policy will be circulated to all schools and departments of the _____ Public Schools and incorporated in staff and student handbooks. It will be posted in the main office and in all faculty lounges. Training sessions on this policy and the prevention of sexual harassment shall be held annually for all staff members and students in all schools.

Student Policy

Students, too, should have their own handbooks that are distributed annually. It is important that all students new to the district also be given a copy of the policy and grievance procedure. More than one adult, a male and a female staff member, should be designated as the person to hear student grievances. Students unfamiliar or uncomfortable speaking with these staff members should be encouraged to talk to any staff member whom they trust. A sample student policy follows.

Sample Sexual Harassment Policy and Procedure for Students[62]

I. Sources of the Policy
  Sexual harassment is forbidden by federal as well as state law. In particular, Title IX of the Education Amendments prohibits discrimination on the basis of sex for all educational programs that receive federal funding. State criminal law, as well as civil law, such as laws against child abuse, all prohibit sexual harassment.

II. The Policy
   A. It is the policy of the _____ Public Schools to maintain a learning and working environment that is free from sexual harassment. No employee or student of the district shall be subjected to sexual harassment.
   B. It shall be a violation of this policy for any student of the _____ Public Schools to harass another student or any staff member through conduct or communications of a sexual nature as defined in Section III. It shall also be a violation of this policy for staff members to harass students or other staff members through conduct or communications of a sexual nature as defined in Section III.
   C. Each administrator shall be responsible for promoting understanding and acceptance of, and assuring compliance with, state and federal laws and board policy and procedures governing sexual harassment within his or her school or office.
   D. Violations of this policy or procedure will be cause for disciplinary action.

III. Definition
   A. Sexual harassment means unwelcome sexual advances, requests for sexual favors and other verbal or physical conduct of a sexual nature from teachers, other adults, students or anyone else the victim may deal with in school, school-related activities, or on the job. It is sexual harassment when:
      1. submission to such conduct is made either explicitly or implicitly a term or condition of a student's participation in school programs or activities;
      2. such conduct has the purpose or effect of unreasonably interfering with or creating an intimidating, hostile, or offensive learning environment.

   B. Sexual harassment, as set forth in Section III-A may include, but is not limited to the following:
      1. Unwelcome sexual behavior
         --verbal harassment or abuse, in person or by telephone
         --non-verbal suggestive pictures, sounds, or gestures
         --sexual name-calling, spreading sexual rumors
         --leers, staring
         --pressure for sexual activity or dates
         --repeated remarks to a person, with sexual implications
         --unwelcome touching, cornering, or other physical contact
      2. Gender-based behavior
         --referring to girls as "foxes," "chicks," "bitches"

--making statements about girls or boys based on gender stereotypes, "It's time for George to go to his cosmetology class; don't you want to fix your make-up first, George?"

--suggesting girls or boys are unable to perform certain work because they lack necessary qualities: "Now, you girls will find calculus harder than boys do."

3. Behavior interfering with school progress

--hiding a girl's tools in auto mechanics class, sabotaging her experiments in physics class

--denying or limiting girls' access to educational tools and experiences, such as computers and other equipment

C. Sexual harassment may be overt or subtle. Some behavior which is appropriate in a social setting may not be appropriate in the school. But whatever form it takes, verbal, non-verbal or physical, sexual harassment can be insulting and demeaning to the recipient and will not be tolerated in the school.

IV. Procedures

A. Any student who alleges sexual harassment by a student or staff member in the school district may complain directly to a teacher, guidance counselor, or administrator [or supply specific personnel designated to hear complaints]. Initial investigations of complaints will begin within 48 hours.

B. The right to confidentiality, both of the complainant and of the accused, will be respected consistent with the school district's legal obligations and with the necessity to investigate allegations of misconduct and to take corrective action when this conduct has occurred.

V. Retaliation

Filing of a grievance or otherwise reporting sexual harassment will not reflect upon the individual's status, nor will it affect future grades, class standing, placement, or recommendations. Complaints of retaliation will be investigated and meritorious complaints will be punished.

VI. Disciplinary Action

A. A substantiated charge against a student in the school district shall subject that student to disciplinary action which may include reprimands, detention, suspension or expulsion, consistent with the student discipline code. A harasser may also be held legally liable under state civil and criminal law.

B. A substantiated charge against a staff member in the school district shall subject such staff member to disciplinary action, including warnings, reprimands, suspension or dismissal. A harasser may also be held legally liable under federal and state anti-discrimination laws and under the criminal laws of this state.

VII. Notification

Notice of this policy will be circulated to all schools and departments of the _____ Public Schools and incorporated in staff and student handbooks. It will be posted in the main office, in the guidance office, and in the cafeteria. Training sessions on this policy and the prevention of sexual harassment shall be held for teachers and students in all schools on an annual basis.

Education of Faculty and Staff

Surveys

A school district working to eliminate sexual harassment can begin by surveying school personnel as well as students to see whether a problem exists in the schools. All personnel should be surveyed, including the custodial staff, bus drivers, security guards, cafeteria workers, secretaries, teachers, and administrators. The results of that survey can be tallied by a team composed of administrators, teachers, and other school personnel. The purpose of the survey should be to determine whether sexual harassment is present in the school, to analyze the sources of the harassment, and to use the results to plan in-service and other staff education programs.

It is important that staff members know that the administration takes a firm stand on sexual harassment and intends to work toward eliminating it. It is also necessary that the term "sexual harassment" be defined before administering the survey since it is a term that encompasses a variety of behaviors. A sample survey follows:

Sample Staff Questionnaire on Sexual Harassment

The school board of _____ School District is committed to eliminating sexual harassment in our schools. We are attempting to discover whether sexual harassment is a problem in our district. If it is, your answers will help us develop programs to reduce sexual harassment.

We ask that you take a few minutes to answer this questionnaire, put it in the sealed envelope provided, and place it _____. All responses will be treated with confidentiality and you need not place your name on the questionnaire.

Definition:

Sexual harassment is a form of sex discrimination forbidden by the Civil Rights Act of 1964 and Title IX of the Education Amendments of 1972.

Sexual harassment is unsolicited and unwelcome sexual advances, requests for sexual favors, and other verbal or physical conduct of a sexual nature. It is sexual harassment when submission to or rejection of the sexual conduct affects an individual's employment, unreasonably interferes with an employee's work performance, or creates an intimidating, hostile, or offensive work environment.

_____
School

____ ____
Male Female

_____
Date

1. Have you ever been subjected to sexual harassment while you have been employed here?

    Yes   No

2. Circle all that apply. If you have been sexually harassed, was the harasser a(n)

    a. teacher or counselor
    b. administrator
    c. student
    d. non-employee
    e. other employee (explain)

3. Regardless whether you have been sexually harassed, have you ever witnessed or heard of sexual harassment occurring at this school?

    Yes   No

4. If you have witnessed or heard of sexual harassment occurring, who was doing the harassment? Circle all that apply.

    a. teacher or counselor
    b. administrator
    c. student

       d. non-employee
       e. other employee (explain)

5. Who was being harassed by this person/these people?
       a. teacher or counselor
       b. administrator
       c. student
       d. non-employee
       e. other employee (explain)

6. What suggestions do you have for how the school can better deal with problems of sexual harassment?

*(The remaining questions are for those who have experienced sexual harassment at this school.)

7. When was your most recent incident of sexual harassment?
       a. it is occurring now
       b. within the past month
       c. within the past six months
       d. within the past year

8. Circle all that apply. What form did the incident take?
       a. physical actions (pinching, patting, stroking)
       b. verbal actions (sexual comments, jokes, requests for sexual relations, sounds)
       c. written actions (notes, jokes, cartoons, pictures)
       d. telephone calls
       e. other (explain)

9. Circle all that apply. Where did the incident take place?
       a. in an office
       b. in a classroom
       c. in a faculty lounge
       d. outside the school building
       e. other (explain)

10. Circle all that apply. How did you respond after the harassment occurred?
       a. did nothing
       b. told the harasser you disliked his sexual advances
       c. told a friend
       d. told a supervisor

      e. followed the school grievance procedure

      f. filed a grievance with the union

      g. other (explain)

11. Circle all that apply. If you took some action to stop the harassment, what response did you get after you took the action?

    a. Response from person complained to or grievance procedure followed:

      1) you were discouraged by person you consulted from doing anything about it

      2) you were told to handle it yourself

      3) you were given advice on how to handle it yourself

      4) you were transferred to another department or school

      5) the harasser was transferred to another department or school

      6) you were given a poor performance evaluation

      7) complaint was satisfactorily resolved

      8) other (explain)

    b. Response from the harasser toward you:

      1) the harassment stopped

      2) the harassment continued

      3) the harassment got worse

      4) the harasser threatened me

      5) other (explain)

12. How do you think your situation should have been handled?

13. Please give us any additional information or comments about this questionnaire or the problem of sexual harassment.

In-Service Workshops

Just as a sexual harassment curriculum should be implemented for students, in-service workshops should be conducted for all school personnel, including district office staff, other administrators, faculty members, the cafeteria and custodial staffs, bus drivers and all other school personnel. Susan Webb, a professional trainer, suggests that in a corporate setting training should be divided into separate sessions for executive-level management, supervisors, and general-level employees because they all have different responsibilities as well as varying degrees of familiarity with laws pertaining to sexual harassment.[63] A comparable breakdown can be applied to schools. The top school officials should be trained first, followed by other administrators and supervisors. All officials and supervisors need to be informed of laws pertinent to sexual harassment and the potential for individual and school liability. It is likely their training will take less time than other employees since they are more familiar with laws applicable to the school.

If the school district is small, subordinate administrators and supervisors can be trained along with chief officials. However, it is preferable to train supervisors separately since they are in a better position to observe sexual harassment at school, and, theoretically, they are already adept at problem-solving. Because they have the onus of being the first line of defense against harassment, it is incumbent upon supervisors never to give even the suggestion of harassing those whom they supervise. It is best to discourage supervisors and other grievance counselors from dating their subordinates. "Romances gone sour" can lead to allegations of sexual harassment and destroy workplace harmony. As supervisors, their sexual misbehavior can entail liability for the entire school district as well as for their own supervisors. *Quid pro quo* cases of sexual harassment impose strict liability on the school district for harassment by its supervisory employees. In hostile environment cases, too, the school may be held liable for harassment by its supervisors.

Supervisors need a thorough understanding of sexual harassment and must be able to recognize it on sight. They also need to be instructed in how to respond to it. In many cases, supervisors will serve as grievance counselors, either to students or to school staff. They must be able to suggest informal techniques for resolving problems of sexual harassment as well as be able to conduct thorough investigations. Informal resolutions save the district time and resources and are conducive to smoother operation of the school and workplace. Supervisors should be instructed that part of their evaluation will be based on how well they carry out the district's anti-harassment policy.

The school should provide additional training for those supervisors who do not adequately enforce the school's policy.

When selecting those who function as grievance counselors, administrators should choose people who are respected by students, faculty, and other school personnel. Counselors should be articulate and be able to write well. Their names should be posted and included in student and staff handbooks. They should report to an upper level administrator whenever sexual harassment allegations are first made and inform the administration of the disposition of the case. Counselors, too, need periodic evaluation and additional training in techniques for dealing with sexual harassment.

It is crucial that all grievance counselors have special training. This training needs to include examples of the types of sexual harassment problems they are likely to encounter at school. They also need to be informed of applicable laws, investigative techniques, means of dealing with victims of sexual harassment, and follow-up strategies.

Faculty members are usually trained to recognize and to deal with sexual harassment during in-service days allocated throughout the school year or, preferably, on an in-service day prior to the opening of school. Ideally, instruction should not be done in groups so large they become unwieldy or in which participants cannot respond. In some districts that will mean training can be done in individual schools. Support staff may, likewise, be trained together. Trainers are unanimous that the initial notice sent out to inform employees of the training session should be brief, straightforward, and should inform employees that the training is mandatory. The notice sets the tone for the entire training program.

The first training session on sexual harassment for each group should be introduced by the head administrator in the school. This administrator should clearly establish the position the school district is taking on sexual harassment, emphasize the significance of the issue, and ask that differing opinions be respected. Trainers also agree that this administrator should introduce the trainer in order to stress the importance with which the school district regards the training. The school cannot expect to change attitudes with a single training session. As Webb says in her book, *Step Forward*, "The primary emphasis of sexual harassment training should be on behavioral changes on the job, and secondarily on attitudinal changes."[64] In this context, employees often have as much or more effect in changing each other's attitudes than trainers do. School districts will have less success if they attempt to imply that sexual harassment is a social, moral, or feminist problem. Webb states that the emphasis should be on the costs to the work environment and legal liability.

Resources

A school district planning to implement sexual harassment workshops for its employees may be unfamiliar with the resources available. Examining the programs used in other school districts is a useful starting point; the district may want to appoint a committee to look into existing programs. Administrators or school counselors may be familiar with such programs. An increasing number of prepackaged programs, usually consisting of films or videos, are available for rental or for purchase. Many women's groups and special interest groups have audio-visual materials available free or at low cost. Leaders often present a video, then conduct group discussion. Contacting groups, such as the state's Commission on Women or the local NOW chapter, can lead to other resources. Materials prepared by the University of Minnesota and the Center for Women Policy studies, for example, may be used to stimulate discussion. (Ordering information is listed in the Appendix, Selected Resources.)

Private consultants who conduct programs on sexual harassment are listed in the yellow pages of the telephone book. Often coordinators at the school's central office conduct workshops, or they know of others who do. The State Department of Education may be able to suggest resources. School districts can also take advantage of their state's Office of Civil Rights or Office of Human Rights. These agencies provide free in-service training throughout the state to corporate offices, government agencies, and other employers who request it. However, since state human rights agencies are also the policing agencies for Title VII and other related federal and state laws, many school districts are reluctant to use them for in-service instruction. Schools that are near colleges or universities can usually avail themselves of that college's library resources. Women's Studies departments may also be able to provide speakers or to suggest other resources.

Contents and Methods

Training programs generally begin with a description of sexual harassment and train staff members in recognizing it. For example, a video may illustrate gender-demeaning comments and inappropriate remarks. One purpose in the early stages of education is to help participants become aware of the many forms sexual harassment takes. Programs encourage employees to distinguish among these forms and to develop strategies for intervention. Employees are also instructed about the myths that perpetuate sexual harassment, the differences between males and females in their perception of harassment, and the laws and liability that apply to harassers. The effect that harassment has on the victims as well as on the school is part of the instruction. A self-scoring pretest is sometimes used to let employees know how their values and perceptions of sexual harassment compare with those of other people in general and with those of the school district in particular. Trainers try to use hypothetical situations that typically focus on problems that have arisen or could arise in the school setting, not only between supervisors and employees but also between co-workers. They then discuss means of dealing with the harassment, eliciting suggestions from program participants. If small groups are used, program leaders may use role-playing to sensitize group members to sexual harassment. One technique is for the instructor to demonstrate a skill intended to teach, for example, how to respond to a sexually harassing comment. Participants will then role-play, attempting to incorporate the skill that has just been modeled. Instructors sometimes use case studies, followed by discussions. Participants may be asked at what point in the example they first noted sexual harassment and are asked to suggest strategies for dealing with it. Teaching coping strategies also shifts the focus away from blaming the victim. Trainees learn how they can support victims of harassment rather than blame them. They also learn assertiveness techniques for dealing with unwanted advances. In general, the more involvement there is from participants, the more effective the training is.

A necessary follow-up to the initial in-service program is the distribution of the school district's sexual harassment policy. Enough time needs to be allowed for an explanation of the policy, discussion of it, and the opportunity for participants to ask questions. After staff members have had time to think about their in-service program and to discuss the district's policy, follow-up sessions should be held during additional in-service training days or faculty meetings so that employees can ask questions and offer suggestions for dealing with sexual harassment.

Education of Students
Surveys

In some schools, sexual harassment does not appear to be a problem. As one high school principal challenged, "Well, look around our building--do you see any sexual harassment?" High school boys and girls were holding hands in the halls, caressing each other in the cafeteria. All the advances seemed welcome. But the lack of sexual harassment may be in the eye of the beholder. A school that has not explained sexual harassment to its students, that has no policy against it, nor a grievance procedure for reporting it will not receive many complaints from students. Ironically, many teachers and administrators prefer it that way. They believe that by calling attention to sexual harassment the school is merely recategorizing inoffensive behavior or behavior that is personal between a boy and girl. They fear that providing information about sexual harassment will lead to the creation of a crisis and that they will be deluged with unfounded complaints. What they don't see is that their failure to adopt a non-discriminatory policy can lead to liability not only for the school district but for themselves as well.

The majority of teachers and administrators, however, want to prevent discrimination--whether it is based on race, national origin, religion, or sex. As a first step in determining whether sexual harassment is a problem in a school, distributing a questionnaire can be helpful. It should be administered to all students, but only after the term "sexual harassment" is defined and the students know that the administration as well as the teachers treat the subject seriously. The questionnaire can be given out during homeroom or in the class where the sexual harassment policy will be explained. It is important that the survey be read to those students who are poor readers. A team of faculty, counselors, students, and an administrator can tally the results, which should then be analyzed and may be used in developing a policy and a grievance procedure. The results can also be used to develop a curriculum or classroom instruction in sexual harassment. A sample student survey follows:[65]

Sample Student Questionnaire on Sexual Harrasment

Sexual harassment may occur between students and teachers and among students. There are laws to protect you, a student, if sexual harassment occurs in school. All information provided by you on this questionnaire is confidential. The more accurate information we have about the threat and reality of sexual harassment to students, the better able we will be to prevent it from occurring.

For questions with more than one answer, please circle as many as apply.

Please indicate your sex: Male   Female

_____   ____   ____
     School   Age   Grade

1. Are you aware of sexual harassment going on in your school among students?

                Yes   No

   among students and teachers?   Yes   No

2. How often do you think instances of sexual harassment occur in this school? Circle all that apply.
    a. all the time
    b. most of the time
    c. once a week
    d. once a month
    e. less than once a month
    f. never

3. Circle all that apply. Have you ever been sexually harassed by
    a. a student(s)
    b. teacher or counselor
    c. coach
    d. administrator
    e. other school staff (explain)

*(The remaining questions are for those who have experienced sexual harassment from a student, teacher, or other school personnel.)

4. In your most serious experience of sexual harassment at this school, how did you feel about the attention?
    a. angry
    b. scared
    c. confused
    d. ashamed
    e. embarrassed
    f. other (explain)

5. What form did the sexual attention take?
    a. staring
    b. gestures or sounds
    c. pulling at clothes

  d. touching, patting, pinching
  e. saying things to me or to others
  f. sexual notes or pictures
  g. asking for sexual activities
  h. other (explain)

6. Where did the attention take place?
  a. classroom
  b. parking lot
  c. in the hall
  d. cafeteria
  e. gym or locker room
  f. on a school bus
  g. on a school trip, away from school
  h. other (explain)

7. When did it take place?
  a. after school
  b. before school
  c. between classes
  d. during class
  e. during lunch
  f. on the weekend or at night
  g. other (explain)

8. Who else was present when the harassment occurred?
  a. no one
  b. a teacher
  c. an administrator
  d. other student(s)
  e. other (explain)

9. Whom did you tell about this incident?
  a. friend
  b. teacher or other staff member
  c. parent
  d. other (explain)

10. What action did you take about the harassment?
  a. none
  b. stayed away from him/her
  c. stayed out of class a few days

    d. changed my class to another one
    e. talked alone to harasser
    f. physically hit the harasser
    g. reported him/her
    h. other (explain)

11. If you reported him/her, to whom did you report?
    a. teacher
    b. administrator
    c. counselor
    d. other (explain)

12. How did you feel about the action you took when the person harassed you?

13. How do you feel now about the harassment?

14. Did the way you responded to the harasser change the relationship you had with him/her?
                Yes   No

15. If you went along with the harasser, what were your main reasons for doing so?
    a. I was scared not to.
    b. I was too confused to do anything or didn't know what to do.
    c. I need to stay on the good side of this person because

    _____.

    d. She/he was popular with the other students.
    e. Other (explain)

16. Did the harasser in any way threaten you if you did not go along with him/her?
                Yes   No
    If so, how?

17. Does this person continue to sexually harass you?
                Yes   No

18. How do you think a situation like sexual harassment should be handled in the school?

19. Please give us any additional information or comments about this questionnaire or the problem of sexual harassment.

Instruction: Developing a Curriculum

Developing an educational program to prevent sexual harassment calls for a comprehensive approach involving more than one type of activity. As a precaution, however, it should be noted that a program that works in one school will not necessarily work in another. It is best to adapt those portions of existing programs that suit the needs of a particular school. As suggested in *Sexual Coercion* by Elizabeth Grauerholz, "Any reforms aimed at schools must examine the social world of young people and take the cultural context of schools into account. Moreover, educators need to be sensitive to racial, ethnic, social class, and environmental differences (for example, rural or urban) when designing and implementing specific programs in schools." [66]

Each school district needs to develop its own curriculum guide so that teachers will be uniform in their instructional approach and to prevent duplication of work that has already been done. Two curriculums in use at the present time are listed in the Appendix, Additional Reading. Whether a sexual harassment curriculum will be mandatory or optional in the schools may depend on state statutes or district policy. Time and money spent on implementing a school-wide curriculum can be saved later by having to spend less time disciplining students and by having fewer grievances that end in lawsuits.

Where in the school day to institute a sexual harassment unit is best left to individual schools. If all students will be studying the unit, then the best place to implement it is in a course all students take. Science, social studies, health, physical education, or English may be classes where the curriculum will fit in. Other possibilities include courses in career planning, psychology, sociology, or an activities period. It is important that each school have the goals it seeks to accomplish with the curriculum firmly in mind. For example, the school district will undoubtedly want to inform students about their legal liability and the school's liability, the causes and effects of sexual harassment, and the school district's policy and grievance procedure for reporting harassment.

Beginning classes in a sexual harassment unit generally focus on defining the term and distinguishing between harassment and flirting. Students can usually arrive at a consensus that flirting makes you feel good and is mutual, whereas sexual harassment produces humiliation and is unwanted by one party. Many students have been sensitized by the media through newspaper and magazine articles, television dramas, and after-school specials, and may be fairly sophisticated about the nature of sexual harassment. It is less likely they can articulate the effect of harassment on the victim and the harm it actually causes.

After sexual harassment is defined, most teachers use a series of activities in which all students are encouraged to participate. The class may be divided into small groups and each group asked to list instances of sexually harassing behavior they have seen in their school. They may distinguish between the behaviors that are more like flirting and those that are more like harassment. Discussion then follows about differences in perception between boys and girls regarding sexual harassment and the sources of rules people make for themselves. Other activities may include student surveys of myths and realities about sexual harassment, followed by discussions; a presentation of the school policy on discrimination in general and sexual harassment in particular; or case studies of harassed students and strategies for dealing with harassment. Some instructors use role-playing or other forms of dramatic presentation to encourage empathy and understanding of the victim's feelings. Students may bring in sample magazine ads that portray men and women stereotypically. Or they may discuss song lyrics that discriminate against women. During other sessions the class can be divided into small all-male and all-female groups to discuss advantages of being male or female. Males may be asked to argue from the perspective of females and vice versa. Speakers from women's groups and from the business community can address problems with sexual harassment in the workplace. Students are some-times asked to write articles about sexual harassment for the local newspaper or the school newspaper.

At particular risk for sexual harassment are those girls entering vocational classes that have traditionally been filled only with boys. They may face gender-demeaning remarks and other forms of harassment from both students and, occasionally, from the instructor. Some boys may be resentful that girls are in the class and be abusive and derogatory toward them. To help girls identify the problems that can arise in vocational classes and to encourage them to develop strategies to deal with harassment, support groups can be created. Support groups consist of an adult--such as a guidance counselor--and a peer group--girls in the same or similar classes who support and advise each other. The main advantage of the support groups has been that they have encouraged girls to stay in vocational classes that they might otherwise have dropped.

Additional suggestions for creating effective programs appear in the Massachusetts curriculum guide, *Who's Hurt and Who's Liable* (See, Additional Reading). Among the suggestions are:

1) Begin discussions of sexual harassment by soliciting examples from students who have observed or have been the subject of harassment in their own school. Later parts of the curriculum can address sexual harassment in the workplace.

2) Be sure students are familiar with the definitions of sexual harassment and have discussed prevailing myths regarding women and harassment.

3) Create a classroom atmosphere in which differences between students and between teachers and students are recognized and respected.

4) Train students, particularly males, as co-leaders. Their presence in the classroom helps defuse anxiety and defensiveness.

A further suggestion, adapted from techniques used by a child abuse counselor, can be used in either a classroom or with a small group. Invite students who were sexually harassed and who subsequently confronted their harasser, filed a grievance, or followed another successful procedure, to come to the class or meet with the group. They may be the best teachers to describe how they felt about the harassment and to tell about the actions they took that were effective and the actions that were unsuccessful. It is also useful for students confronting sexual harassment to see that others experience similar problems, face them, and overcome them.

Education of Families and the Community

Title IX mandates that the parents of elementary and secondary school students be notified that the school does not discriminate on the basis of sex in its educational programs or activities.

> Each recipient [of federal funds] shall implement specific and continuing steps to notify applicants for admission and employment, *students and parents of elementary and secondary school students*, employees, sources of referral of applicants for admission and employment, and all unions or professional organizations holding collective bargaining or professional agreements with recipient, that it does not discriminate on the basis of sex in the educational programs or activities which it operates, and that is required by title IX and this part not to discriminate in such a manner.
> 34 C.F.R. 106.9(a) (1990) (emphasis added)

In addition to the distribution of handbooks to all students and staff members, the school has various means at its disposal to inform parents and other community members of its non-discrimination policy. Local newspapers and magazines are media suggested by Title IX regulations. Schools can also use their student newspapers to feature articles on sexual harassment in the local schools and in schools throughout the U.S. Articles that focus on cases in other school districts would be informative to families in the district. Many schools send home monthly or quarterly newsletters in which the policy can be included. Information can also be disseminated through Parent-Teacher organizations, at "Open House" events, and at other school functions. Numerous other handouts are sent home by schools--by booster clubs, athletic organizations, and social clubs. Each of these is a potential resource for disseminating the school's non-discrimination policy. Public service announcements on radio and television will also provide the community with information about the policy.

Resistance from parents to discussions of sexual harassment in classrooms and the implementation of a curriculum educating students about sexual harassment has been prevalent in some school districts. Parents may fear talking about the subject will increase incidents of harassment or that it will lead to false accusations. Other parents, with moral objections, reject any mention of sex at school, whether it is in regard to sex education or sex discrimination. Educating these parents on the law and the necessity of complying with state and federal requirements may be difficult, but Title IX clearly mandates that all parents be informed of the school's anti-discrimination policy.

Monitoring the School Campus
Vocational Departments/Vocational Schools
A place where girls are frequently subjected to sexual harassment is in the vocational school or in the vocational department of their schools. Although girls may enjoy the work in a carpentry or auto repair program and are aware of the career opportunities resulting from completion of such courses, they frequently decline to enroll in these programs. One reason is they are often made to feel uncomfortable in vocational classes. The instructor may "joke" about the "ladies" in his class and overlook what he considers the "pranks" of the boys. He may directly or indirectly encourage gender-baiting. Boys may directly harass the girls--by namecalling, by placing obscene drawings and cartoons in their toolboxes, by hiding their materials, by fondling them.

At the same time, the harassment may take more subtle forms. In one machine shop in a vocational school, a large poster was tacked to a wall facing students as they walked in. Purportedly stressing the proper clothing to be worn in class, the poster depicted a tall blonde-haired woman. The bottom of the poster was blocked off, but the top portion showed the woman from the shoulders up, apparently naked. "Jeans are for play," was the caption written across the bottom.

Classes in which girls feel uncomfortable or intimidated or in which they feel they must defend themselves on a daily basis are not classes in which they will enroll or in which they will remain if they do enroll. Providing in-service "sensitivity" training for instructors, a curriculum on sexual harassment for the students, and support groups for female class members will help reduce incidents of sexual harassment. One of the objectives of Title IX is to insure that all students have equal access to school programs. Stating that all students may enroll in any program is not the same as facilitating that enrollment and making sure that students and faculty comply with the school's non-discrimination policy. It is the duty of vocational instructors and school administrators to see that girls and boys who enter vocational classes are not bullied or intimidated into withdrawing from them. Unless the faculty and administration eliminate sexual harassment, students will not have equal access to all school programs.

Restrooms and Classrooms

Restrooms are one of the most common places to find written evidence of sexual harassment. Derogatory graffiti can appear in either boys' or girls' restrooms, and it can be hard to uncover unless someone notifies the person about whom the graffiti is written or unless the school is attentive to it.

In one school, offensive graffiti describing several of the girls began to appear in the boys' restrooms. The principal appointed one custodian to clean the walls of each restroom at the end of the day. The graffiti re-appeared each day for the next several months, but the custodian tenaciously pursued his job. Finally, the principal surmised, the graffiti-writer must have tired of his vandalism and given up. No further graffiti appeared for the rest of the year.

Within the classroom, faculty should be responsible for periodically checking walls and desk tops for graffiti. A once-a-week cleaning of desk tops can be accomplished in five minutes by students and teacher working together. After giving each student a paper towel, the teacher moves throughout the room spraying desk tops with liquid cleanser. Each student wipes his own desk. One student circulates, collecting the used paper towels.

The cafeteria and hallways are also places where sexual harassment is likely to occur. Teachers and administrators must be trained to recognize sexually harassing behavior when they see and hear it. They need to explain to the offending student how his behavior violates the school non-discrimination policy. If the offensive behavior persists, they should follow the disciplinary procedure the school uses in other cases of misbehavior.

The school must respond quickly when harassing graffiti appears. In the case of Katy Lyle, the graffiti persisted throughout her high school years, even though her parents continued to inform administrators at their daughter's school about it. Unless the school promptly removes the damaging graffiti, it can incur liability for its inaction.

Outside the School Building
Working to eliminate sexual harassment is the responsibility of all school personnel. Administrators should not be the only "enforcers." For example, coaches working on the athletic fields with students after school should not tolerate the sexual harassment of those students. Girls on the track team should not be subjected to the comments and catcalls of boys watching them from the stands. Nor should boys be subjected to this type of harassment. The coach is the person who should speak to those

students and tell them he welcomes their support for the team, but that they must either stop their harassing behavior or leave.

Busdrivers should be instructed to report instances of sexual harassment to the administration. Offending students should be reprimanded and, ultimately, denied access to school-furnished transportation if they refuse to stop sexually harassing other students.

The exterior of the school buildings, the most visible portion of the school, should be the responsibility of everyone in the school--all students as well as all school personnel. Students should be urged to report to administrators or to remove offensive graffiti when they see it. Employees can do the same. As often as the graffiti appears, it must be removed. A school that delays removing the harassing messages or does it incompletely increases its liability in proportion to the slowness and the ineptitude with which it acts.

What Can the School Do If Sexual Harassment Occurs?

Informal vs. Formal Grievance Procedures: Definitions

Despite a clear and widely disseminated sexual harassment policy and despite training of both staff and students, incidents of sexual harassment will occur. It is important to have a procedure in place whereby complaints can be handled quickly and appropriately.

Grievance procedures generally fall into two categories: informal and formal. Informal procedures place the responsibility on the complainant to attempt to negotiate an end to the harassment by confronting the harasser candidly and directly. One reservation some trainers have is that since no penalties are involved in informal resolution of sexual harassment, the danger exists that the harasser will not see the seriousness of his behavior. The fear of some counselors is that the harasser may continue his behavior--the next time with a more cooperative victim. However, unless the harassment is severe, a victim who can put a stop to it herself by using informal means faces less emotional turmoil and develops greater confidence in her ability to take care of her own problems. There is also less disruption in the school. Informal procedures are likely to end the offensive behavior. Often the harasser will be incredulous that his behavior constitutes sexual harassment, and he will immediately cease his harassment.

Formal procedures are more adversarial and require the filing of a written complaint, investigation, and a factual finding of guilt or innocence. These procedures are time-consuming and can be traumatic for both harasser and victim. In addition, they can be disruptive in the workplace and in the classroom. They frequently force friends and co-workers to take sides, pit students against students and staff members against each other. The institution of formal proceedings against a harasser leads to rumors and gossip in the community and, invariably, negative publicity for the school. However, if the harasser is uncooperative and unwilling to stop the harassment, the school district must not only provide formal grievance procedures, but they must also see that they are implemented promptly.

A strong guidance and support system for the victim is a necessary component of an effective sexual harassment program. The methods of informally confronting a harasser, described in the next section, apply to staff members as well as to students.

A student or staff member who confides an instance of sexual harassment to a grievance counselor wants several things: 1) she wants to know what can be done to make the harassment stop, 2) she wants assurance that her complaint will be treated confidentially, 3) she wants reassurance that she did the right thing by reporting the incident to the counselor, 4) she wants to be sure there will be no repercussions or retaliation for relating the incident. It is important that her complaint be taken seriously by the listener. From the standpoint of comforting the complainant as well as from decreasing liability, it is imperative that the school district act quickly in handling the complaint: it should respond within 48 hours or less.

Informal Grievance Procedures

Once the complainant contacts a designated grievance counselor and alleges that she is being sexually harassed, the school should adhere to its previously announced procedures. First, the grievance counselor should take notes on the complaint made, being as specific as possible. She should record the date, statements made, and action suggested. Those notes should be kept in locked files (not in the student's permanent record file to which others in the school have access). It is important to assure the complainant that her charge will be treated with confidentiality. Assuming that the charge is not severe (for example, it does not involve touching, threats of harm, or has not occurred over a long period of time), the counselor should suggest informal means for the victim to deal with the harasser. The complaint should be recorded on a standard form. (See sample below.)

If a student is complaining of the behavior of a staff member, the grievance counselor should notify the principal immediately. Students should not be advised to handle sexual harassment by a staff member on their own. Should the allegation involve charges of child abuse, it is mandatory for teachers, counselors, and administrators in most states to report the incident to the state protective agency that handles child abuse. Child abuse should also be reported to local law enforcement agencies as well. In a recent case involving a teacher who propositioned a student, fondled her, and exposed himself to her, the school delayed over a week before informing the police. States often have laws mandating that any crime that occurs on a school campus must be reported to the police immediately. Delay in taking action contributes to school liability.

School administrators should thoroughly investigate charges of sexual harassment by an employee, carefully documenting how they conducted the investigation and the action they took. It is important for the investigator to comply with the district's grievance procedure or collective bargaining agreement.

A sample grievance form might contain the following:

Sexual Harassment Report Form

Name of complainant _____

Date _____

Person(s) accused of harassment _____

Date(s) incident occurred _____

Location of incident _____

Description of incident

Witnesses to incident

Impact on complainant

Suggested course of action

Follow-up

I certify that the information is true and complete to the best of my knowledge.

_____   _____
(Complainant's Signature)   (Counselor's Signature)
                              _____
                              (Title)

Informal Methods of Handling Sexual Harassment

When advising a student or employee to deal with the harasser on her own, the counselor should give the complainant specific suggestions. Some ways of handling sexual harassers are listed below.

Take Notes

Advise the complainant to write down all instances of sexual harassment, including the time and location, and place them in chronological order. She should indicate other people who may have witnessed the harassment. She should also state how she responded to the harasser--whether she ignored him or spoke to him. Students may not be clear about what has happened to them, other than to say they were made to feel "uncomfortable." Encourage complainants to describe, with precision, the details of the behavior that made them feel uncomfortable. If they can remember the words of the harasser or the gestures he used, it will be useful to record them. The advantage of putting the complaint in writing is that it helps the victim clarify the incident in her own mind. It also gives the victim a perspective on the incident. By writing it down, some details may be seen to be of lesser or greater importance than the complainant originally thought. An additional advantage is that the complainant now has a record of the event and can readily refer to dates and details should she need them in the future. She should be told to save any notes, drawings, or other writing that the harasser gave her.

Confront the Harasser

After the complainant has a clear idea in her own mind of the behavior she objects to, she should confront her harasser and tell him of her objections. The counselor should encourage her to speak to him in person at a time when others are not around. She should describe in detail the behavior she objects to and where and when it occurred. She should tell the harasser how she feels about the behavior and tell him she wants it to stop. A further suggestion is that she state a course of action she will take if the harassment does not stop. It is a good idea to advise the complainant to practice her "speech" so that she feels comfortable saying it. For example, she might be advised to say:

Example: Student Confronting a Harassing Student
> Mike, last Friday in geometry class when I was working on an assignment, you pretended to be drawing on my back with your pencil. Then you began playing with my hair and tried to braid it. After I asked you to stop, you still continued to twist my hair. I felt uncomfortable and embarrassed by what you did and I couldn't concentrate on my work. Please stop touching me or I will ask Mr. Krueger to change your seat.

Example: Secretary Confronting Harassing Administrator
> Jack, I think you mean to be funny, but I don't like the sexual cartoons and jokes that you've put on my desk. Twice this week after lunch you placed them on my desk as you winked and walked by. I want you to stop giving me these "jokes" since they offend me and I don't think they're funny at all.

For students who find it too difficult to confront the harasser alone, some authorities advise taking a friend or a trusted adult along. Besides providing moral support, the friend can also confirm, should it be necessary later, that the victim told the harasser his advances were unwelcome.

Have Someone Else Confront the Harasser
In the event a complainant is unwilling or unable to confront the harasser herself, she may ask a grievance counselor to have a talk with him. A secretary may ask the principal or another administrator to speak to the offender about his behavior.

The advantage of this method is that it eliminates the need for confrontation between victim and harasser, it is confidential, and it avoids the formal grievance procedure. If the incident is minor and if the harasser is amenable to change, a short talk may be all that is necessary to remedy the harassment. The offender may not have realized his advances or his comments were unwelcome. On the other hand, a victim who refuses to complain to the offender must rely on others to speak for her and forgoes the opportunity to develop confidence in her ability to deal with problems on her own.

Write a Letter to the Harasser

A slightly different technique, but one which uses content similar to the oral complaint, is writing a letter to the harasser. The technique was suggested by Mary P. Rowe, writing in the *Harvard Business Review* (May-June 1981). Letter-writing can supplement an oral complaint that has not produced results, or it can take the place of the oral confrontation. The letter should be non-threatening, yet precise in its details. Rowe suggests that it have three parts:

Part I - Write a factual account of what happened, without coloring the account with personal feelings. The account should contain as many details about the incident as the victim can remember. For example: "After school Thursday when I went to track practice, you and your friends were sitting in the stands hollering comments and crude suggestions. While I was jumping hurdles you yelled, "Boy, I'd like her to jump on me!"

Part II - The writer describes how she feels about the events described in Part I, such as disgusted, sad, or embarrassed. For example: "When I heard you yell, I was humiliated and could not concentrate on my event. As a result, I felt I did poorly."

Part III - The writer states what she wants to happen next. This part is usually short. For example: "I want you to stop yelling at me during track practice or stop coming to practice at all."

The writer signs and dates the letter, making sure to keep a copy for herself. If she needs it later, it will help her document the incident. The original should be delivered in person or by certified mail. The grievance counselor may ask to keep a copy as well.

The victim may find that the harasser was not even aware that his behavior was offensive. He may be concerned that the victim has showed the letter to others or that she is planning to follow through with the grievance procedure. In most cases, the harassment will stop after the harasser receives the letter. Should the harasser want to discuss the incident further, the victim is not bound to accommodate him. She can reiterate that she just wants the harassment to stop.

The advantages of writing a letter may be summarized as follows:

1) it helps the victim regain a sense of being in control of the situation;
2) it often avoids formal charges and a public confrontation;
3) it keeps the incident(s) confidential;
4) it provides the harasser with a new perspective on his behavior;
5) it may minimize or prevent retaliation against the writer;
6) it is not necessary to address questions such as legality, confidentiality, evidence and due process; and
7) it usually works.[67]

Talk to Others

It is often suggested that a person who is sexually harassed talk to others--usually those in a position similar to herself--to see whether they, too, have been harassed. It is always helpful to have corroborating witnesses. As a group they can then present a united front and build a stronger case against their harasser. Seeking out other victims is a good idea where the person harassed has witnessed or has heard of the harassment of other victims. In one case, six high school girls complained together about a male science teacher who was harassing them. The school took note of and acted on their complaint.

However, it is probably best to be discreet and not to go on a "fishing expedition" when attempting to find others who have been harassed. The plan can backfire as rumors spread throughout the school and the complainant loses her shield of anonymity.

Formal Grievance Procedures

Any allegation of sexual harassment that cannot be resolved informally or any allegation of sexual harassment by a student against an adult requires measures that are more thorough and formal. Most important, once the school becomes aware that a grievance has been filed, it must investigate charges promptly and take disciplinary action quickly against the harasser.

Investigations of Employees Charged With Sexual Harassment

Harassment of Students by Teachers and Other School Employees

Reports to administrators of sexual harassment by an employee may come from numerous sources. If the employee is a teacher, other faculty members who have witnessed his harassing behavior may notify an administrator. Students may confide in a teacher or counselor, who should know that any threat to student welfare must be reported to the administration. Counselors need to tell students that in cases of more serious abuse, physical touching for example, the counselor may need to file a report with the state's child protective service agency as well. In other cases, teachers may overhear students talking or find notes they have written that refer to sexually harassing behavior. Sometimes the report comes from an irate parent or group of parents. Regardless of the source of the report, the school must follow its grievance procedure or collective bargaining agreement when investigating such reports.

Occasionally, an outside organization, such as a law enforcement agency, will notify the school of its investigation of sexual misconduct of an employee--for illustrative purposes, suppose the harasser is a teacher. Although the school must cooperate with the law enforcement agency, it can still conduct its own investigation, and it may be wise for the school district to do so. If the law enforcement agency drops the charges against the teacher or the teacher plea bargains to a lesser charge, school officials may be left without a course of action if they were depending on the agency to do their investigative work for them. By the time the school begins its belated investigation, witnesses may have moved and memories have dimmed. Because the school district is not bound to the court's standard of criminal culpability--"beyond a reasonable doubt"--if it has conducted its own investigation and has found even a lesser degree of guilt, it can still take disciplinary job action against the teacher, including dismissal. Information gathered by law enforcement officials will be available to the school.

Trained building administrators or district-level administrators should conduct the investigation. It is preferable for the interviewer to be the same sex as the complainant. Some districts may prefer an independent investigator, such as the school district's attorney. Whoever is chosen should have experience conducting investigations, should be knowledgeable about sexual harassment, should be analytical and objective, and should know her responsibilities. She should also be aware that she must observe any collective bargaining agreement. She should keep her supervisor informed at each stage in the investigation.

Nancy J. Hungerford, in an article in *School Law in Review 1991*, lists a series of steps that are helpful in conducting an investigation.[68]

Step One

1) The first step is to interview the student who is making the allegations. The investigator must be careful not to prompt the witness but to let her tell her own story. Parents should be informed beforehand that the interview will take place. However, she should be interviewed without her parents present, if district policy permits, to insure that her testimony will remain more credible should there be a later hearing. Regardless of district policy about including parents during an interview with

their child, the setting should be private and another counselor or administrator should be present. The second person can take notes or ask questions the first administrator may have omitted. Preferable to note-taking is tape recording the interview.

In addition, a standard form (such as that in the section on Informal Grievance Procedures) should be used as a permanent record of the interview. The investigator must get specific names, dates, places, and a description of the objectionable behavior. It is helpful to have a set of prepared questions that are open-ended and non-leading. The questions should be designed to elicit specific information and not require a perfunctory "yes" or "no" answer. The investigator should avoid asking "why" questions and compound questions. The claimant should also be asked about her response or reaction at each stage of the harasser's conduct.

Once the student has given the details of the incident the National School Boards Association's Council of School Attor-eys[69] suggests that the interviewer not discourage a student complaint with words such as: "It will just be your word against his," "Do you see how this makes you look?", "Do you know what could happen to Mr. X?" Furthermore, a student's promiscuous or seductive behavior is legally irrelevant to her charges of sexual harassment against the alleged harasser. Her prior behavior may not be used as a defense to a school's failure to act on the complaint.

The Council also cautions that the alleged harasser may be extremely popular and an unlikely perpetrator of sexual harassment. As a result, a school may be reluctant to investigate charges out of loyalty to the staff member. The staff member may be defensive and it is unlikely he will admit he made sexual advances. Even after being convicted of sexual harassment in a court of law, the harasser may deny he made sexual advances, or he may deny his advances were unwelcome. Regardless of the popularity of a staff member and regardless how unlikely the charges against him may be, the school will be held liable for its failure to investigate the allegations.

Hungerford suggests that students be asked broad, general questions, such as, "Has anything happened to you at school recently that has caused you to be upset?" rather than asking about a specific action that a teacher took. If the student is reticent, the investigator must be prepared to ask more specific questions, yet she must not suggest answers to her own questions. It is important that the student, as well as the investigator, sign the complaint form.

The administrator should stress that she will attempt to keep the matters discussed private. Students need to confide in friends, but they also need to be cautioned that details of the investigation should not be discussed with students other than those involved since it may jeopardize the investigation. The school district needs to keep in mind that discretion in its investigation may prevent later problems, such as charges of defamation, by the alleged harasser. To that end, it is better to have only one person handle all typing and filing.

The student should be told how the investigation will be conducted and given a time frame for each step. She needs to know she may be interviewed again and that she will be advised of the conclusions of the investigation. Once the investigation has begun, students and their parents need to be apprised of each step taken by the counselor.

If the initial report of harassment comes from a parent, it is in the interest of the interviewer to find out when his child first made the allegation, what the atmosphere in the home was at the time, and whether other students have been told of the harassment. Sometimes the complainant will later retract an allegation. Administrators are advised to continue their investigations, even against the wishes of the complainant. It may be that the student fears embarrassment if the incident becomes known by other students. She may also have been threatened or coerced to drop her charges.

If the charges against the teacher are serious, he will most likely be suspended with pay. At this time he needs to be told of the general allegations against him and informed that an investigation will take place.

Step Two

2) Follow-up interviews of those students mentioned by the accuser as having been present during the sexual harassment are the next step. It may also be useful to interview those witnesses who were in a position to observe the complainant immediately after the harassment occurred. All witnesses should be asked about only those incidents of which they have personal knowledge. Each of these students should be interviewed, one at a time and within a time frame when it will not be possible for them to talk to each other before being interviewed. Hungerford suggests asking all persons interviewed to draw a diagram showing "who was where" during critical time segments. They should also provide a detailed time sequence describing the episodes and the amount of time they lasted. To prevent the spread of rumors throughout the school and the community, students should be asked to discuss the investigation only with their parents. Each student interviewed should be asked to sign her statement.

Step Three

3) The investigator then interviews the alleged harasser and explains the complaints against him. Prior to this meeting, the investigator needs to review all statements of students plus any other "evidence" she may have--notes, drawings, and correspondence from the accused teacher. It would also be a good idea to review the teacher's personnel file as well as the student's file for any information that might corroborate or contradict the charge. The teacher should be informed at the outset that the school district treats allegations of sexual harassment seriously. The charges against the teacher must contain dates, times, and places of alleged incidents. At this stage, depending on the gravity of the charges, the teacher may have an attorney and/or a union representative present. The teacher should provide a

signed, written statement, which may be presented by his attorney. The teacher may willingly provide an explanation for the alleged harassment, deny the charges, or confess that they are accurate. If he denies the charges, he should be asked if he knows any reason why these charges may have been made against him.

The employee is told the district may need to investigate further, but that it will inform him of the action it intends to take as quickly as possible. The interviewer may solicit names of persons the employee wants the school district to interview.

Step Four

4) The school district then completes its investigation, reviews all the evidence, and determines promptly which, if any, charges can be substantiated with solid evidence. If the charge is substantiated, the complainant and the defendant should be notified in writing as to the action the district will then take. The school district should use care in following its own policies and those of the collective bargaining agent to safeguard the rights of the alleged harasser. If additional counseling is needed by the victim, the school should provide it.

If a serious charge has not been proven, an employee may still be disciplined for a lesser infraction. He should also receive a written reprimand that contains a warning that if the behavior is repeated, the teacher will be discharged. He should be counseled about the nature of the problem and clearly told of the behavior expected of him. State law and the local collective bargaining agreement will determine whether dismissal or discipline is the proper action. Appropriate sanctions depend on the type and severity of the offense and whether the employee has been disciplined before for a similar charge. In some cases where "immorality" has not been proved, a teacher may still be dismissed under a statute proscribing "neglect of duty." The school district should prepare a written report of the investigation and maintain it in a separate file, not in the employee's personnel file.

If allegations of sexual harassment have not been proved, the employee must be notified in writing at once. The student who complained should also be informed in writing of the out-come of the investigation and of any right to appeal. The employee needs to get back to work without being subjected to further rumors and innuendo. If the district does not indicate that it has cleared its employee, the employee is likely to sue the school for defamation. In cases in which a reprimand, but not a dismissal, is given, the investigator must follow up on the case. Periodic interviews with the student should take place to insure there is no recurrence of the harassment.

Harassment of Non-School Workers by Employees
A similar type investigation must be conducted when em-ployees of the school harass non-school personnel. In these cases the school district may not have access to witnesses if the sexual harassment occurred off the school premises. The district may have to place more reliance on police reports and other information gathered by law enforcement agencies. Also, if the harassment did not occur during the school day, in order to dismiss the employee, the district must show there was a connection between the act committed and the ability of the employee to perform his job at school. The establishment of this connection is frequently included in collective bargaining agreements.

Harassment of Employees by Supervisors
Employees should know the names of the counselors to whom they can turn in case of sexual harassment. The names of counselors should be posted as well as listed in the employee handbook. An employee who has tried informal means of resolv-ing harassment by a supervisor, who is unable to confront her harasser, or whose harassment is severe or pervasive needs to consult her grievance counselor. As in the case of a sexually harassed student, the allegation should be investigated carefully.

With the exceptions for those procedures applicable to minors, a similar method is used to investigate supervisors.

1) The counselor interviews the employee and gets a signed detailed statement signed by both the employee and the counselor.
2) Witnesses named by the employee are interviewed and also give a signed statement.
3) The counselor interviews the alleged harasser and records his signed statement.
4) The counselor completes his investigation and the school makes a disposition commensurate with its findings. The school may reprimand the employee, dismiss him, or impose a lesser penalty.
5) The counselor follows up on the case to see there is no recurrence of the harassment nor retaliation against the complainant.

After allegations of sexual harassment against an employee have been resolved, it is in the best interest of the school district to analyze the incident to see how future incidents can be avoided. The school district may need to write its sexual harassment policy more clearly or conduct training sessions to sensitize its employees to sexual harassment. It may need to review its grievance procedure to see if the incident could have been handled more efficiently.

Harassment of Students by Peers

By all accounts, harassment of students by their peers is the most pervasive form of sexual harassment. The 1993 poll of 1,632 students in grades 8-11 taken for the American Association of Union Women (AAUW) reported that 80% of the unwelcome behavior is by students and directed at other students. In one study of junior and senior high school students in Chaska, Minnesota, a majority of females had experienced sexual harassment at school.[70] The AAUW poll showed 65%

of girls and 42% of boys polled reported they had been touched, grabbed, or pinched in a sexual way. The behaviors reported most frequently were sexual comments, including name-calling; staring/leering; inappropriate touching and gestures. According to the survey, the locations where sexual harassment most frequently took place were in the classroom and in the hallway. However, comments and contact can occur anywhere--on the bus, on the athletic field, in the cafeteria, and in the media center.

Unless the harassment is severe or involves sexual contact, students should informally try to resolve unwanted sexual advances themselves. (See the preceding section of this book, Informal Grievance Procedures.) Speaking to the harasser or sending him a letter are usually effective ways to put a stop to sexual harassment. Serious harassment that involves assault should be immediately reported to the principal, to the police, and to the state children's protective services agency. No student should attempt to cope by herself with a harasser who threatens physical assault.

In other cases, when informal resolution fails, the school must initiate a thorough investigation. The following steps are similar to those used when complaints are made against adults.

1) The administrator, after notifying the student's parents, interviews the student alleging that sexual harassment has occurred; she may state that her efforts to stop it, by speaking to the offender or by writing a letter have failed. The administrator sets the tone of the meeting by telling the student that sexual harassment is treated as important, that the district has a firm policy against it and will not tolerate it. She is assured that her confidentiality will be respected.

The counselor records, in detail, all the offenses the student is alleging, including the location, time, nature of the incident, witnesses, and her response to the harasser. Both student and counselor sign the statements. Similar questions to those asked in cases of harassment by a teacher may be asked (See Harassment of Students by Teachers and Other School Employees).

2) Corroborating witnesses suggested by the complainant are interviewed and their signed statements are taken.

3) The parents of the alleged harasser are informed their child will be interviewed. During the interview the student is told the school district has a firm policy forbidding sexual harassment. The allegations are explained. The student is given the opportunity to tell a version of the incident, and a signed statement is taken.

4) After the school completes its investigation, it informs both the alleged harasser and the victim in writing of the results of its investigation and the action the school will take. If a report is founded, depending on the gravity and pervasiveness of the harassment and whether the harasser has been disciplined before for making sexual advances, the school should promptly discipline the harasser. Such discipline may take the form of a written apology to the victim, counseling, suspension, or, after a hearing, expulsion.

In the case of employee harassment by co-workers, the interview process is the same, absent notice to parents, and the disciplinary action may take the form of reprimands, apologies, counseling, or dismissal.

Follow-Up Actions Schools Can Take
Implementing a sexual harassment policy and grievance procedure is only the initial step to eliminating sexual harassment. The school district must remain committed to its goals of preventing harassment, dealing with cases of sexual harassment promptly, and following up to insure there is no recurrence or retaliation against complainants. To this end, the school must keep abreast of changes in statutes and case law that affect the area of discrimination by keeping in contact with the school dis-

trict's attorneys. Some follow-up activities need to be carried out on a daily basis; some, only periodically, or as needed; and others, annually.

Daily Actions

On a daily basis administrators must continue to make clear to students and personnel that the school will not tolerate sexual harassment. Without that unequivocal message from the chief administrators, an anti-harassment policy is likely to fail. The message becomes clear when the principal announces the policy to the staff and to the students, when allegations of sexual harassment are dealt with quickly, and when the discipline of harassers is prompt and consistent.

Administrators and other school personnel also get the message across by their own actions--by not ignoring sexual harassment in the halls and in the classroom and by setting an example through their own behavior. Supervisors, especially, have a duty to express their objection to sexually harassing behavior when they witness it or are informed it has occurred. All school personnel need to speak out when they hear jokes in which the "humor" depends on the denigration of people based on their gender, race, religion, handicap, or national origin. Psychologists sometimes suggest that those who want to express disapproval of offensive jokes use an "I" rather than a "you" statement. "I just don't find jokes that make fun of blondes amusing" is preferable to, "You think blondes are really stupid, don't you?"

It is a mistake to make sexual harassment a "women's issue." That is done when the development of a policy is left entirely to female faculty members, and remediation of offenders is left solely to female guidance counselors or assistant administrators who "have a talk with" the offender. Making it a women's issue conveys the message that only women are bothered by sexual harassment and that the issue is not very important. The first line of defense in implementing a policy is the top administrators who present a conspicuous, unified front against sexual harassment.

Administrators also need to monitor the halls, restrooms, and classrooms for offensive graffiti, posters, and drawings. Particular attention needs to be paid to vocational schools or to vocational portions of buildings where sexually harassing posters and drawings are likely to be prevalent. Graffiti on the outside of buildings is readily observable. Discriminatory materials need to be removed. Supervisors in various parts of the school building can be held liable for tolerating sexual harassment. If they witness sexually harassing behavior in a school bus parking lot, for example, or in the students' parking lot, they have a duty to confront the harasser and take steps to end the offensive behavior.

At the same time, teachers must encourage students and employers must encourage their employees to speak up and not be coerced by perpetrators of sexual harassment. The school district should consider offering assertiveness training or counseling groups for students who are unwilling to stand up to their harassers. They need to be taught to articulate the specific behavior that offends them and to learn informal as well as formal procedures for dealing with that behavior.

Periodically or As Needed

The school should continue to offer in-service programs to sensitize its employees to issues of sexual harassment. Participants should critique the programs and offer suggestions for improving them. The student curriculum should be updated periodically and new means of drawing attention to sexual harassment found, whether it is through articles in the school newspaper, a poster contest, or "speak-outs" on the topic.

Victims of sexual harassment should be supported and encouraged to report their harassers. Once it is determined that allegations of sexual harassment are true, the harasser should be disciplined fairly and similarly to others who commit comparable acts. The student and her family should be kept informed of the action the school will take against the harasser. If a move to another class or building is required, it is usually best to remove or transfer the sexual harasser rather than his victim. Transferring the victim implies that she is to blame for the harassment and that the school is partial to the harasser. The counselor needs to follow up in cases of sexual harassment to insure there is no retaliation against the victim or recurrence of the harassing behavior.

Annually

School districts must keep all employees and students informed of any changes in the laws and in recent case law relating to sex discrimination. Parents, students, and school personnel should receive copies of the sexual harassment policy, the grievance procedure, and the names of counselors to contact for advice or in order to file a complaint. To monitor the effectiveness of their policies and procedures, the district can administer annual, follow-up surveys to those who have reported being sexually harassed. Students and employees should be asked to evaluate the handling of their case and to suggest means of improving both policy and procedure. An annual report should be made in which the number of complaints and the disposition of complaints are tabulated. This will help the district assess the effectiveness of its policy and procedure. Grievance counselors need to be kept aware of effective intervention strategies for dealing with harassment and, when possible, attend workshops outside the school district.

Wanting to minimize adverse publicity regarding a teacher who has sexually harassed students, school districts may retain the teacher and attempt to bargain with the victim. The district may agree to transfer the harasser to another school within the district in order to induce the victim to abandon legal proceedings. Although the harassment may then stop for that victim, it will usually recur in the school where the harasser is transferred. Schools must dismiss employees who, despite reprimands and the imposition of more severe disciplinary measures, continue to sexually harass students or employees. Whenever possible, the school district also needs to warn potential employers of the harassing behavior of their former employees.

However, warning potential employers about employees creates a dilemma for employers. When a sexual harasser is dismissed from a school district and applies in another district, school officials of the new district may be unaware of his offensive behavior. The school district that continues to give favorable recommendations to perpetrators of sexual harassment insures the continued victimization of students and employees. Furthermore, failure to inform the new school district of a sexual harasser's activities can increase the likelihood of liability for the school district. On the other hand, school districts are becoming reluctant to relay negative evaluations of their former employees to prospective employers because they fear incurring liability for defamation. Increasing numbers of lawsuits have been won by former employees who have been denied employment based on the unfavorable evaluations of previous employers.

The extent to which a school district may inform a prospective employer about the sexually harassing behavior of its former employee is unsettled. Of course, the outcome of any suit brought in a court of law may be communicated to a prospective employer. However, when no suit has been brought, some employers are willing to acknowledge in writing only that the employee formerly worked in the school district but that he is no longer employed there.

Employers must provide accurate information that conforms with applicable agreements or laws. Facts may be transmitted, but the employer should avoid conclusions of guilt or his opinions regarding the former employee if he wishes to avoid a suit for defamation.

Schools can also take preventive measures when hiring new employees to insure the reliability of candidates. They should thoroughly verify the references furnished, including those of part-time employees and substitutes. Reference checks should be documented and maintained. The employment application should be reviewed with the applicant and any questionable response discussed with him. Where state laws permit, an applicant's criminal record should be inspected, and the state's child abuse registry should be examined for a possible match. The applicant's teaching license or certificate should be verified. Applicants can be asked to sign a waiver releasing former employers from liability for disclosing personnel records and evaluations. Finally, until all background and employment information has been verified, the applicant should not be offered employment.[71]

Avoiding Liability, Providing Equal Access
to an Equal Education

School officials who deny that sexual harassment exists or who believe the problem is trivial fear that discussion of sexual harassment will open a floodgate of unfounded complaints. They believe women and girls will re-characterize behavior formerly described as joking or amorous "play" as sex discrimination. They are apprehensive that men and boys who intended no harm will have to endure disciplinary action and damaged reputations. Administrators' time will be wasted on petty grievances.

The danger in refusing to enforce laws against sexual harassment is that personal and district-wide liability can result. However, legal liability is only one form of harm that results from the toleration of sexual harassment. Another, and even greater harm, is the damage done to girls when they are denied an equal opportunity for an education. A girl subjected to constant peer harassment or daily gender harassment from a teacher cannot be an equal participant in the school program. The school that refuses to take a stand on sexual harassment sends a message that girls are of lesser value than boys. Girls interpret the inaction to mean that the school denies gender equality, that adults are not to be trusted, and that the world at-large is an unjust place. It is crucial, therefore, that schools take the necessary steps to minimize, if not entirely prevent, sexual harassment.

Inspiring and enabling girls to do their best in the classroom not only helps individual girls, it also helps future generations. As the AAUW report points out, most girls will become mothers. "Higher levels of education among mothers play an important role in reducing poverty among children. . . .Inadequate education not only lowers opportunities for women, but jeopardizes their children as well. Given the increase in the number and percentage of women who are single parents and the growing importance of women's wages to total family income, the education of women is important not only for women as individuals, but also for women as mothers, as family members, and as effective and creative citizens of larger communities."[72] To achieve those goals, some observers believe that it will be necessary to "change the culture of schools" and to focus on "the creation of substantive change" rather than on the reduction of liability.[73]

One important step schools can take now toward the equitable education of women is to eliminate sexual harassment. Bringing the topic into the "mainstream of education" is necessary. This can only be done by decisive, committed school leaders who will implement an anti-discrimination policy and a grievance procedure that is accessible to all students and school personnel. Developing long-range goals and marshaling all available resources will enable staff members to be productive employees. It will also enable female students to participate equally in the education to which they are entitled.

Appendix I
Selected Resources

9 to 5, National Association of Working Women
614 Superior Avenue, NW
Cleveland, OH 44113
(216) 566-9308
(800) 522-0925 (Hotline)
National, non-profit organization with local affiliates. Provides publications, legal referrals, and free, confidential information and advice on work-related concerns, including sexual harassment. Trained counselors provide advice (see hotline number, above). See *The 9 to 5 Guide to Combating Sexual Harassment*. pap. $9.95.

American Federation of State, County, and
    Municipal Employees (AFSCME)
1625 L Street, NW
Washington, DC 20036
(202) 429-5090
Publishes booklet on how to stop sexual harassment (available only to members of AFSCME). Training workshop for members.

American Federation of Teachers (AFT)
Human Rights Department
555 New Jersey Avenue, N.W.
Washington, DC 20001

(202) 879-4000
Publication on sexual harassment available to union members.

BNA Communications, Inc.
Department AFC-022
9401 Decoverly Hall Road
Rockville, MD 20850
(301) 948-0540
"Preventing Sexual Harassment." Part of BNAC's *Fair Employment Practice* program. 51-minute video for managers, 15-minute employee version. 24-hour preview available.

Bureau of Educational Resources and Television
Massachusetts Department of Education
75 Acton Street
Arlington, MA 02174
(617) 727-6395
"No Laughing Matter: High School Students and Sexual Harassment." Slide/tape presentation of three high school girls who encounter sexual harassment in school and at work. Discussion of strategies to prevent and eliminate sexual harassment.

California Commission on the Status of Women
926 J Street
Room 1506
Sacramento, CA 95814
Help Yourself: A Manual for Dealing with Sexual Harassment. Includes all aspects of sexual harassment and contains selected list of resources. Primarily aimed at California residents, but useful for anyone who wants more information about sexual harassment.

Center for Occupational Education
Jersey City State College
2039 Kennedy Boulevard
Jersey City, NJ 07305

(201) 547-2188
(800) 272-7837
"Sending the Right Signals: A Training Program About Dealing with Sexual Harassment." Materials include video and student handbook on sexual harassment. Program is intended to educate, teach communication techniques, and provide information about legal rights.

Center for Sex Equity in Schools
SEB 1046
University of Michigan
Ann Arbor, MI 48109-1259
(313) 763-9910
Curriculum and guide available for use with high school students. Gives examples of sexual harassment in high school, suggestions for support groups and activities, and strategies for administrators to address the problem.

Center for Women Policy Studies
2000 P Street, N.W., Suite 508
Washington, D.C. 20036
Center is a research and advocacy institution for women. Catalogue of publications available, including packet on sexual harassment.

Clark Communications
943 Howard Street
San Francisco, CA 94103
(415) 777-1668
"The Workplace Hustle." 20-minute film narrated by Ed Asner focuses on sexual harassment in white collar jobs. Available through The Network, Inc., Andover, MA (617)470-1080.

Gamma Vision, Inc.
119 South Main
Suite 330

Seattle, WA 98104
(206) 682-9552
"Sexual Harassment in the Schools." 15-minute slide/tape show on sexual harassment in secondary and vocational schools. Includes Title VII and Title IX law, case studies, methods of resolving sexual harassment problems.

Lifeguides
KCET Video
4401 Sunset Boulevard
Los Angeles, CA 90027
(800) 343-4727
"Sex, Power and the Workplace." Hour-long video + 22-p. resource guide. Video narrates instances of sexual harassment in the workplace, interviews women who have brought suit against their employers, and gives the results of those cases (including *Ellison v. Brady*). Intersperses commentary by attorneys, employers, and advocates for women.

MTI Teleprograms, Inc.
3710 Commercial Avenue
Northbrook, IL 60062
(800) 323-5343
Available through MVCRC, Lexington, MA (617)863-1863.
"The Power Pinch: Sexual Harassment in the Workplace." 28-minute film illustrating examples of sexual harassment in the workplace. Uses role-plays and legal explanations. For school personnel and some high school classes.

National Education Association (NEA)
Human and Civil Rights Department
1201 16th Street, N.W.
Washington, DC 20036
(202) 833-4000
Videos and other publications on sexual harassment available to NEA members. Contact local affiliate for more information.

Now Legal Defense and Education Fund
99 Hudson Street
New York, NY 10013
(212) 925-6635
Legal Resource Kit on Employment - Sexual Harassment
Kit provides general information, primarily on legal aspects
of sexual harassment.

Penn State Audio-Visual Services
Special Services Building
University Park, PA 16802
(814) 865-6314
(800) 826-0132
"The Wrong Idea," a cross-cultural training program about
sexual harassment. Contains a 20-minute video tape and training
manual with nine vignettes portraying incidents of sexual
harassment in the classroom and on campus. Purchase, rental,
preview available.

Programs for Educational Opportunity
University of Michigan
1005 School of Education
Ann Arbor, MI 48109-1259
*Tune in to Your Rights: A Guide for Teenagers about Turning Off
Sexual Harassment*. Booklet suggests strategies for dealing with
problems of sexual harassment. $3.00.

Wellesley College Center for Research on Women
Publications Department
106 Central Street
Wellesley, MA 02181-8259
(617)283-2510
Offers publications, such as *Secrets in Public: Sexual Harassment
in Our Schools*. Results of a joint project of NOW Legal
Defense and Education Fund and the Center for Research on
Women, 1993. 23pp. $11.00.

Appendix II
Minnesota State Statute:
Sexual Harassment and Violence Policy

Minnesota law requires each school district to adopt a policy prohibiting sexual harassment and sexual violence. Victims may file grievances with the school district and with the Minnesota Department of Human Rights. An individual may also initiate a civil suit. Sanctions are provided both for those who perpetrate sexually harassing behavior and for those who make false allegations that are frivolous or harassing in intent. Chapter 127.46 of the Minnesota State Statues now reads:

Each school board shall adopt a written sexual harassment and sexual violence policy that conforms with sections 363.01 to 363.15 [Minn. State Human Rights Act]. The policy shall apply to pupils, teachers, administrators, and other school personnel, include reporting procedures, and set forth disciplinary actions that will be taken for violation of the policy. Disciplinary actions must conform with collective bargaining agreements and sections 127.27 to 127.39 [policies under the Education Code]. The policy must be conspicuously posted throughout each school building and included in each school's student handbook on school policies. Each school must develop a process for discussing the school's sexual harassment and violence policy with students and school employees.

Appendix III
State Civil Rights Agencies

The following civil rights agencies are state agencies. Most accept complaints about discrimination in employment (Title VII) based on sex, age, race, ethnicity, handicap, and religion. Many agencies also take complaints about discrimination in housing and public accommodations. Some take complaints based on hate crimes. Starred agencies (*) process complaints based on discrimination in education. In addition, larger cities and some counties have their own civil rights agencies to receive complaints. Consult state agencies for further information.

Alaska Human Rights Commission
800 A St., Suite 204
Anchorage, AL 99501
(907) 276-7474; (907) 276-3177(TDD)

Arizona Civil Rights Division
1275 West Washington St.
Office of the Attorney General
Phoenix, AZ 85007
(602) 542-5263

Minority Affairs
Office of the Governor
State Capitol #238
Little Rock, AR 72201

California Department of Fair Employment
    and Housing
2014 T St., Suite 210
Sacramento, CA 95814-6835
(916) 739-4621; (916) 739-4638 (TDD)

Connecticut Commission on Human Rights
    and Opportunities
90 Washington St.
Hartford, CT 06106
(203) 566-4895

District of Columbia Department of
    Human Rights & Minority Business
2000 14th St., N.W.
Washington, DC 20009
(202) 939-8740; (202) 939-8793 (TDD)

Delaware Department of Labor
Labor Law Enforcement Section
820 North French St.
6th Floor
Wilmington, DE 19801
(302) 577-2882

Florida Commission on Human Relations
325 John Knox Rd.
Suite 240, Building F
Tallahassee, FL 32303-4102
(904) 488-7082; (904) 488-7082 (TDD)

Georgia Commission on Equal Opportunity
710 Cain Tower, Peachtree Center
229 Peachtree St., NE
Atlanta, GA 30303
(404) 656-1736

Hawaii Civil Rights Commission
888 Mililani St., 2nd Floor
Honolulu, HI 96813
(808) 586-8636

Idaho Human Rights Commission
450 West State St.
Boise, ID 83720
(208) 334-2873

Illinois Department of Human Rights
100 West Randolph St., Suite 10-100
Chicago, IL 60601
(312) 814-6200; (312) 814-1579 (TDD)

Indiana Civil Rights Commission*
Indiana Government Center North
100 North Senate, N103
Indianapolis, IN 46204
(317) 232-2600; (317) 232-2629 (TDD)

Iowa Civil Rights Commission
211 East Maple Street, 2nd Floor
Grimes State Office Building
Des Moines, IA 50319
(515) 281-4121

Kansas Human Rights Commission
900 Southwest Jackson, Suite 851-South
Topeka, KS 66612-1258
(913) 296-3206; (913) 296-0245 (TDD)

Kentucky Commission on Human Rights
322 West Broadway, 7th Floor
Louisville, KY 40202
(502) 595-4024

Louisiana Commission on Human Rights
P.O. Box 94094
Baton Rouge, LA 70814

Maine Human Rights Commission
State House - Station 51
Augusta, ME 04333
(207) 624-6050; (207) 624-6064 (TDD)

Maryland Commission on Human Relations
20 East Franklin St.
Baltimore, MD 21202-2274
(410) 333-1717; (410) 333-1737 (TDD)

Massachusetts Commission Against Discrimination
Asburton Place, Room 601
Boston, MA 02108
(617) 727-3990

Michigan Department of Civil Rights*
303 West Kalamazoo
Lansing, MI 48913
(517) 335-3164; (313) 961-1552 (TDD)

Minnesota Department of Human Rights
500 Bremer Tower
7th Place & Minnesota St.
St. Paul, MN 55101
(612) 296-5663; (612) 296-1283 (TDD)

Missouri Commission on Human Rights
3315 W. Truman Blvd.
P.O. Box 1129
Jefferson City, MO 65102-1129
(314) 751-3325; (314) 444-7590

Montana Human Rights Commission*
P.O. Box 1728
Helena, MT 59624
(406) 444-2884

Nebraska Equal Opportunity Commission
301 Centennial Mall South, Fifth Floor
Lincoln, NE 69509
(402) 471-2024

Nevada Equal Rights Commission
1515 E. Tropicana, Room 590
Las Vegas, NV 89119
(702) 486-7161

New Hampshire Commission on Human Rights
163 Loudon Rd.
Concord, NH 03301-6053
(603) 271-2767

New Jersey Division of Civil Rights
31 Clinton St.
Newark, NJ 07102
(201) 648-2700

New Mexico Department of Labor
Human Rights Division
1596 Pacheco St., Aspen Plaza
Santa Fe, NM 87502
(505) 827-6838

New York State Division of Human Rights
55 West 125th St.
New York, NY 10027
(212) 870-8794

North Carolina Human Relations Commission
121 West Jones St.
Raleigh, NC 27603
(919) 733-7996; (919) 733-7996 (TDD)

North Dakota Department of Labor
600 East Blvd., 6th Floor
Bismarck, ND 58505-0340
(701) 224-2660

Ohio Civil Rights Commission
200 Parsons Ave.
Columbus, OH 43266-0543
(614) 466-2785; (614) 466-9353

Oklahoma Human Rights Commission
2101 North Lincoln, Room 480
Jim Thorpe Building
Oklahoma City, OK 73105
(405) 521-3441

Oregon Bureau of Labor and Industries
Civil Rights Division
800 N.E. Oregon St., #32, Suite 1070
Portland, OR 97232
(503) 731-4075; (503) 731-4106 (TDD)

Pennsylvania Human Relations Commission
101 South Second St., Suite 300
Harrisburg, PA 17101
(717) 787-4410; (717) 783-9308

Department of Labor and Human Resources
505 Munoz Rivera Ave., 14th Floor
Hato Rey, PR 00918
(809) 754-5806

Rhode Island Commission for Human Rights
10 Abbot Park Place
Providence, RI 02903-3768
(401) 277-2661; (401) 277-2664

South Carolina Human Affairs Commission
P.O. Box 4090
2611 Forest Dr., Suite 200
Columbia, SC 29204
(803) 253-6336; (803) 253-4125 (TDD)

South Dakota Division of Human Rights
222 East Capitol St., Suite 11
Pierre, SD 57501-5070
(605) 773-4493

Tennessee Human Rights Commission
Cornerstone Square Building, Suite 400
Nashville, TN 37243-0745
(615) 741-5825

Texas Commission on Human Rights
P.O. Box 13493
Austin, TX

Utah Labor and Anti-Discrimination Division
160 East 300 South
Salt Lake City, Utah 84111-0870
(801) 530-6801

Vermont Attorney General's Office
Civil Rights Division
109 State Street
Pavilion Office Building
Montpelier, VT 05609-1001
(802) 823-3171

Virgin Islands Department of Labor
P.O. Box 148
Charlotte Amalie
St. Thomas, VI 00804
(809) 775-3498

Washington State Human Rights Commission
711 South Capitol Way, Suite 402
P.O. Box 42409
Olympia, WA 98504-2490
(206) 753-6770

West Virginia Human Rights Commission
1321 Plaza East, Room 106
Charleston, WV 25301-1400
(304) 558-2616; (304) 558-2976 (TDD)

Wisconsin Equal Rights Division
Department of Industry, Labor and Human Relations
P.O. Box 8928
201 East Washington Ave., Room 40
Madison, WI 53708
(608) 266-6860

Wyoming Department of Employment
Labor Standards Division
Herschler Building
122 West 25th St.
Cheyenne, WY 82002
(307) 777-7261

Appendix IV
Office for Civil Rights
Regional Offices

The following regional offices accept discrimination complaints based on race, color, national origin, sex (Title IX), handicap, or age in educational institutions or programs receiving federal assistance. Free copies of technical assistance resource material pertaining to discrimination may be obtained by writing to:

> U.S. Department of Education
> Office for Civil Rights
> Mary E. Switzer Building, Room 5000
> 400 Maryland Avenue, S.W.
> Washington, D.C. 20202

Region I Connecticut, Maine, Massachusetts, New Hampshire, Rhode Island, Vermont
> Office for Civil Rights, Region I
> U.S. Department of Education
> J.W. McCormack Post Office and Courthouse
> Room 222, 01-0061
> Boston, MA 02109-4557
> (617)223-9662
> (617)223-9695 (TDD)

Region II New Jersey, New York, Puerto Rico, Virgin Islands
    Office for Civil Rights, Region II
    U.S. Department of Education
    26 Federal Plaza
    33rd Floor, Room 33-130, 02-1010
    New York, NY 10278-0082
    (212)264-4633
    (212)264-9464 (TDD)

Region III Delaware, District of Columbia, Maryland,
  Pennsylvania, Virginia, West Virginia
    Office for Civil Rights, Region III
    U.S. Department of Education
    3535 Market Street, Room 6300, 03-2010
    Philadelphia, PA 19104-3326
    (215)596-6772
    (215)596-6794 (TDD)

Region IV Alabama, Florida, Georgia, North Carolina, South
  Carolina, Tennessee
    Office for Civil Rights, Region IV
    U.S. Department of Education
    Post Office Box 2048, 04-3010
    Atlanta, GA 30301-2048
    (404)331-2954
    (404)331-7816 (TDD)

Region V Illinois, Indiana, Michigan, Minnesota, Ohio,
  Wisconsin
    Office for Civil Rights, Region V
    U.S. Department of Education
    401 South State Street, Room 700C, 05-4010
    Chicago, IL 60605-1202
    (312)886-3456
    (312)353-2541 (TDD)

Region VI Arkansas, Louisiana, Mississippi, Oklahoma, Texas
Office for Civil Rights, Region VI
U.S. Department of Education
1200 Main Tower Building, Suite 2260, 06-5010
Dallas, TX 75202-9998
(214)767-3959
(214)767-03639 (TDD)

Region VII Iowa, Kansas, Kentucky, Missouri, Nebraska
Office for Civil Rights, Region VII
U.S. Department of Education
10220 North Executive Hill Boulevard, 8th Floor
Kansas City, MO 64153-1367
(816)891-8026
(816)374-6461 (TDD)

Region VIII Arizona, colorado, Montana, New Mexico,
North Dakota, South Dakota, Utah, Wyoming
Office for Civil Rights, Region VIII
U.S. Department of Education
Federal Building, Suite 310, 08-7010
1244 Speer Boulevard
Denver, CO 80204-3582
(303)844-5695
(303)844-3417 (TDD)

Region IX California
Office for Civil Rights, Region IX
U.S. Department of Education
Old Federal Building
50 United Nations Plaza, Room 239, 09-8010
San Francisco, CA 94102-4102
(415)556-7000
(415)556-6806 (TDD)

Region X Alaska, Hawaii, Idaho, Nevada, Oregon,
Washington, American Samoa, Guam, Trust
Territory of the Pacific Islands
    Office for Civil Rights, Region X
    U.S. Department of Education
    915 Second Avenue, Room 3310, 10-9010
    Seattle, WA 98174-1099
    (206)553-6811
    (206)553-4542 (TDD)

NOTES

[1]MacKinnon, Catherine, *Sexual Harassment of Working Women*, New Haven: Yale University Press (1979), p. 27.

[2]*Williams v. Saxbe*, 413 F. Supp. 654 (D.C.Cir. 1976).

[3]Maypole, D.E., & Skaine, R., "Sexual Harassment in the Workplace," 28 *Social Work* 1983, pp. 385-390.

[4]Pentagon, 1990.

[5]1991, United States Navy.

[6]Dzeich, B.W. & Weiner, L., *The Lecherous Professor: Sexual Harassment on Campus*, Boston: Beacon, 1984, p. 15.

[7]Brown, W.A. & Maestro-Scherer, J., *Assessing Sexual Harassment and Public Safety: A Survey of Cornell Women*, Ithaca: Cornell Institute for Social and Economic Research, July 1, 1986, p. 23.

[8]Salking, E.J., "Can't You Take a Joke?' A Study of Sexual Harassment Among Peers" (Master's Thesis, Massachusetts Institute of Technology, February 1986), p. 63.

[9]*Who's Hurt and Who's Liable: Sexual Harassment in Massachusetts Schools*, Quincy: Massachusetts Department of Education, 1986.

[10]*The A.A.U.W. Report: How Schools Shortchange Girls--A Study of Major Findings on Girls and Education*, Washington: American Association of University Women/National Education Association, 1992.

[11]Hughes, J.O. and Sandler, B.R., "In Case of Sexual Harassment: A Guide for Women Students," Washington: Project on the Status and Education of Women, Association of American Colleges, 1986, p. 3.

[12]"9th Circuit Studies Gender Bias," *American Bar Association Journal*, November 1992, p. 30.

[13]Elizabeth Grauerholz and Mary A. Koralewski, *Sexual Coercion: A Sourcebook on Its Nature, Causes, and Prevention*, Lexington: Heath, 1991, pp. 152-153.

[14]*Id.*, p. 153.

[15]*Id.*

[16]Linn, Eleanor, et al, "Bitter Lessons for All: Sexual Harassment in Schools," in *Sexuality and the Curriculum: The Politics and Practices of Sexuality Education*, James T. Sears, ed., New York: Teachers College Press, Columbia University, 1992.

[17]Id., p. 108.

[18]Jenson, Inger W. and Gutek, Barbara A., "Attributions and Assignment of Responsibility in Sexual Harassment," *Journal of Social Issues*, 38 (1982), pp. 133-34.

[19]*Id.*, p. 154.

[20]Miranda Van Gelder, "High School Lowdown," 2 *Ms.* (March/April, 1992), p. 94.

[21]Salisbury, Ginorio, Remick and Stringer, "Counseling Victims of Sexual Harassment," 23 *Psychotherapy*, No. 2 (1986), p. 318.

[22]Hughes, J.O. and Sandler, B.R., "Peer Harassment: Hassles for Women on Campus, Washington: Project on the Status and Education of Women, Association of American Colleges, 1988, p. 2.

[23]*Id.*

[24]Salsbury, Ginorio, Remick and Stringer, p. 319.

[25]LeBlanc, A.N., "Harassment in the Halls," *Seventeen* (September 1992), p. 164.

[26]Stein, Nan D., "It Happens Here, Too: Sexual Harassment in Schools," *Education Week* (April, 1992).

[27]Gutek, B.A., *Sex and the Workplace*, San Francisco: Jossey Bass, 1985.

[28]Hughes and Sandler, "Peer Harassment," p. 3.

[29]Van Gelder, p. 94.

[30]*Williams v. Saxbe*, 413 F. Supp. 654 (D.C.Cir. 1976).

[31]*Meritor Sav. Bank v. Vinson*, 477 U.S. 57 (1986).

[32]*Henson v. City of Dundee*, 682 F.2d 897 (11th Cir. 1982).

[33]Lindemann, B. and Kadue, D. D., *Sexual Harassment in Employment Law*, Washington: Bureau of National Affairs, Inc., 1992.

[34]*Andrews v. City of Philadelphia*, 895 F.2d 1469, 1485 (3rd Cir. 1990) (quoting *Tomkins v. Public Serv. Elec. & Gas Co.*, 568 F.2d 1044, 1047 n.4 (3d Cir. 1977)).

[35]Adapted from Lindemann and Kadue, *Sexual Harassment in Employment Law*.

[36]*Rabidue v. Osceola Ref. Co.*, 805 F.2d 611 (6th Cir. 1986).

[37]*Robinson v. Jacksonville Shipyards*, 760 F. Supp. 1486 (M.D. Fla. 1991).

[38]The Sixth in Cincinnati, the Seventh Circuit in Chicago, and the Eleventh Circuit in Atlanta.

[39]The Third Circuit in Philadelphia, the Eighth Circuit in St. Louis, and the Ninth Circuit in San Francisco.

[40]Lindemann and Kadue, pp. 168-169.

[41]See, e.g., *Paroline v. Unisys Corp.*, 879 F.2d 100 (4th Cir. 1989), *Hansel v. Public Serv. Co. of Colo.*, 778 F.Supp. 1126 (D. Colo. 1991), *Smolsky v. Consol. Rail Corp.*, 780 F.Supp. 283 (E.D. Pa. 1991), *Sparks v. Regional Medical Center Bd.*, 792 F. Supp. 735 (N.D. Ala. 1992).

[42]*EEOC v. Hacienda Hotel*, 881 F.2d 1504 (9th Cir. 1989).

[43]*Stockett v. Tolin*, 791 F. Supp. 1536 (S.D. Fla. 1992).

[44]*Ellison v. Brady*, 924 F.2d 872 (9th Circ. 1991).

[45]*Alexander v. Yale*, 459 F. Supp. 1 (D. Conn. 1977) and *Alexander v. Yale Univ.*, 631 F. 2d. 178 (2d Cir. 1980).

[46]*Cannon v. University of Chicago*, 441 U.S. 677 (1979).

[47]*Pfeiffer v. Marion Ctr. Area Sch. Dis.*, 917 F.2d 779 (3rd Cir. 1990).

[48]*Franklin v. Gwinnett County Pub. Schools*, ___ U.S. ___, 112 S.Ct. 1028 (1992).

[49]*Id.*, p. 1037.

[50]*Stoneking v. Bradford Area School District*, 822 F.2d 720 (3rd Cir. 1989), cert. denied, *Smith v. Stoneking*, 493 U.S. 1044 (1990).

[51]*D.R. v. Middle Bucks Area Vocational Technical Sch.*, 972 F.2d 1364 (3rd Cir. 1992).

[52]*Kyriazi v. Western Electric Co.*, 461 F. Supp. 894 (D.N.J. 1978).

[53]Adapted from "Memorandum on Sexual Harassment: Sexual Harassment Claims in the Public Sector," Minnesota School Boards Assn. in *Sexual Harassment in the Schools: Preventing and Defending Against Claims*, Washington: National School Boards Association, 1990.

[54]*Tinker v. Des Moines Sch. Dist.*, 393 U.S. 503 (1969).

[55]*R.A.V. v. City of St. Paul*, ___ U.S. ___, 112 S.Ct. 2538 (1992).

[56]*New Jersey v. T.L.O.*, 469 U.S. 325 (1985).

[57]*Id.* at 339.

[58]*Id.*

[59]Survey in *Title IX Line--Center for Sex Equity in Schools*, Univ. of Mich. School of Educ., Ann Arbor, Fall, 1983.

[60]"Sexual Harassment in the Schools: A Statewide Project for Secondary and Vocational Schools," Seattle.: Northwest Women's Law Center, 1986.

[61]*Id.* at 36.

[62]Adapted from *Sexual Harassment to Teenagers: It's Not Fun/It's Illegal*, St. Paul: Minnesota Department of Education, n.d.

[63]*Id.*

[64]Webb, Susan L., *Step Forward: Sexual Harassment in the Workplace, What You Need to Know!* New York: Mastermedia Books, 1991 (See Chapter 5 for training suggestions).

[65]*Id.* at 75.

[66]Adapted from *Sexual Harassment to Teenagers*, pp. 48-52.

[67]Grauerholz and Koralewski, p. 155.

[68]Hughes, Jean O. and Sandler, Bernice R., "In Case of Sexual Harassment: A Guide for Women Students," Washington: Project on the Status and Education of Women, Association of American Colleges, 1986, p. 4.

[69]Hungerford, Nancy J., "Investigating and Screening Sexual Misconduct Charges & Coordination with Other Agencies," *School Law in Review* 1991, Washington: National School Boards Association, 8-1.

[70]Gittins, Naomi E., "Practical Advice on Handling Sexual Harassment in Schools," *Sexual Harassment in the Schools: Preventing and Defending Against Claims*, Washington: National School Boards Association, 1990.

[71]*Sexual Harassment to Teenagers*, p. 11.

[72]Adapted from Gittins, "Practical Advice on Handling Sexual Harassment in Schools," *Sexual Harassment in the Schools: Preventing and Defending Against Claims*, pp. 43-44.

[73]*The A.A.U.W. Report: How Schools Shortchange Girls*, p. 5.

[74]Linn *et al.*, p. 120.

Additional Reading

A.A.U.W. Report: How Schools Shortchange Girls--A Study of Major Findings on Girls and Education. Washington: American Association of University Women/National Education Association, 1992.

Berthel, K. Lee. "Sexual Harassment in Education Institutions: Procedure for Filing a Complaint with the Office for Civil Rights, Department of Education." 10 *Capital University Law Review* 585 (1981).

Black, Beryl. *Coping with Sexual Harassment.* New York: Rosen, 1987.

Crocker, Phyllis L. and Simon, Anne. "Sexual Harassment in Education." 10 *Capital University Law Review* 541 (1981).

Decker, Robert H. "Eleven Ways to Stamp Out the Potential for Sexual Harassment." *American School Board Journal*, August 1988 at 28.

Dziech, Billie Wright & Weiner, Linda. *The Lecherous Professor: Sexual Harassment on Campus.* Boston: Beacon, 1984.

Gittins, Naomi E. and Walsh, Jim, eds. *Sexual Harassment in the Schools: Preventing and Defending Against Claims.* Washington: National School Boards Association, 1990.

Grauerholz, Elizabeth & Koralewski, Mary A., eds. *Sexual Coercion: A Sourcebook on Its Nature, Causes, and Prevention.* Lexington: Lexington Books, 1991.

Kaser, Joyce and Ross, Marlene. "Preventing Sexual Harassment of School Employees." *Educational Leadership*, November 1983 at 53.

Lindemann, Barbara & Kadue, David D. *Sexual Harassment in Employment Law.* Washington: BNA Books, 1992.

Meyer, Mary Coeli, et al. *Sexual Harassment.* Princeton: Petrocelli, 1981.

Petrocelli, William & Repa, Barbara Kate. *Sexual Harassment on the Job.* Berkeley: Nolo, 1992.

Powell, Elizabeth. *Talking Back to Sexual Pressure.* Minneapolis: CompCare, 1991.

Regotti, Terri L. "Negligent Hiring and Retaining of Sexually Abusive Teachers." *Education Law Reporter*, May 21, 1992 at 333.

School Law in Review 1991. Washington: National School Boards Association, 1992.

Sears, James T., ed. *Sexuality and the Curriculum: The Politics and Practices of Sexuality Education*. New York: Teacher's College Press, Columbia University, 1992.

Sexual Harassment in the Schools: A Statewide Project for Secondary and Vocational Schools. Seattle: Northwest Women's Law Center, 1986.

Sexual Harassment to Teenagers: It's Not Fun/It's Illegal (A Curriculum for Use with Junior and Senior High School Students). St. Paul: Minnesota Department of Education, n.d.

Sorenson, Gail P. "Sexual Abuse in Schools: Reported Court Cases from 1987-1990." *Educational Administration Quarterly* (4), 1991 at 460.

Strauss, Susan. "Sexual Harassment in the School: Legal Implications for Principals." *National Association of Secondary School Principals Bulletin*, March, 1988 at 93.

Tannen, Deborah. *You Just Don't Understand: Women and Men in Conversation*. New York: Morrow, 1990.

Underwood, Julie. "End Sexual Harassment of Employees, or Your Board Could be Held Liable." *American School Board Journal*, April 1987 at 43.

Webb, Susan L. *Step Forward: Sexual Harassment in the Workplace. What You Need to Know!* New York: Mastermedia, 1991.

Who's Hurt and Who's Liable: Sexual Harassment in Massachusetts Schools (A Curriculum and Guide for School Personnel). Quincy: Massachusetts Department of Education, 1986.

Winks, Patricia. "Legal Implications of Sexual Contact Between Teacher and Student." *Journal of Law & Education*, 1982 at 437.

Wishnietsky, Dan H. "Reported and Unreported Teacher-Student Sexual Harassment." *Journal of Educational Research*, January/February, 1991 at 164.

INDEX